THE
NEW TESTAMENT WORLD

Insights from cultural anthropology

BRUCE J. MALINA

SCM PRESS LTD

Unless otherwise indicated Scripture quotations are from the Revised Standard Version of the Holy Bible, copyright, 1946, 1952, and 1971, 1973 by the Division of Christian Education, National Council of the Churches of Christ in the USA and used by permission. The italics have been added by the author.

334 02215 0

First published 1981 by John Knox Press, Atlanta
First British edition published 1983
by SCM Press Ltd
26–30 Tottenham Road, London N1

Typeset in the United States of America
and printed in Great Britain by
The Camelot Press Ltd
Southampton

Preface

This book was written in particular for the student beginning to study the New Testament. Its purpose is to present, from the area of cultural anthropology, some useful models that may help in fathoming the social context of the behavior of the people presented in the New Testament. Most New Testament study takes place in terms of verbal and literary analysis, historical description of persons and events, as well as some geographical and archeological information, all of which serve to clarify the meaning of the texts. All such information is certainly of great value for making the Word of God intelligible. However, most of the time students of the Bible take all such information and conceive of it as operating in much the same way as it would operate in our own society. Such unconscious shuffling of cultural contexts might make the Bible immediately relevant to the student, but at what cost to the meaning intended by the author in the first place?

The purpose of using anthropological models in New Testament study is precisely to get to hear the meaning of the texts in terms of the cultural contexts in which they were originally proclaimed. The models chosen for the book are mid-range models in the sense that they serve to explain segments of behavior rather than the whole cultural picture of the social world of early Christianity. Choosing models is based upon presuppositions, and in the first chapter I set out the presuppositions behind model-building in general and cultural anthropology in particular. Models from cultural anthropology do not offer an alternative explanation of the Bible, nor do they do away with literary-critical, historical, and theological study. Rather, they add a dimension not available from other methods, along with a way to check on the hunches of interpreters when it comes to questions of social context.

The models presented here are those which I feel will be most useful for students as they come to grips with the data presented in introductory level New Testament courses. Chapter 2 deals with honor and shame, the pivotal values of Mediterranean culture in antiquity and in the present. Chapter 3 looks to the social psychology of the persons described in our texts; chapter 4 to their implicit perception of all goods as limited; chapter 5 to what they mean by kinship and marriage; and chapter 6 to their purity rules. Throughout the book I have attempted to point out our own implicit assumptions in these areas, thus allowing for a comparative perspective.

In order for the models to generate the understanding they were designed to do, the student must read the New Testament, for this book has been written in a way which makes little sense apart from constant reference to the New Testament writings themselves. Go through the passages listed at the end of each chapter, where I deal with testing models. Look up the biblical passages cited in the course of the chapter. Those coming to the New Testament for the first time should note that, as a rule, sentences in the New Testament that are in the passive voice imply that God is acting. Passive voice means that the grammatical subject of the sentence is being acted upon. For example, "John kicks the horse" is active voice because John, the grammatical subject, does the acting. In "John is kicked", the subject of the sentence, John, is acted upon, and we are not told who is doing the acting. *This is passive voice. Passive voice sentences in the New Testament mean God is the actor or doer.* So, for example, "many are called, few are chosen" means that God calls many (=all), but does not choose all; "to whom much is given" means those to whom God gives much; "all power in heaven and on earth has been given to me" means God has given me all power everywhere.

Good models are meant to explain, guide, reveal and aid discovery. The New Testament passages listed in the exercises as well as the text are by no means exhaustive examples. And not all the suggestions generated by the models have been followed through in the text. The attentive student will find much to add to what is stated in the book, and much to uncover that has not been explicitly pointed to at all. Good models at the introductory level are meant to bring creative insights to the beginner. Perhaps the models presented here will serve that end.

Bruce J. Malina

Contents

1

Bible Study and
Cultural Anthropology

The objective of this book is to sketch out some of the dimensions involved in studying the writings of the Bible for the purpose of gaining some understanding of them on their own terms. What does such a study entail? Suppose you found yourself passing through Syria toward the end of the first century A.D., and as you made your way through some Syrian Hellenistic city, you heard the following words being read aloud as you walked by a somewhat crowded private dwelling:

εἰσὶν γὰρ εὐνοῦχοι οἵτινες ἐκ κοιλίας
μητρὸς ἐγεννήθσαν οὕτως
καὶ εἰσὶν εὐνοῦχοι οἵτινες εὐνουχίσθησαν
ὑπὸ τῶν ἀνθρώπων
καὶ εἰσὶν εὐνοῦχοι οἵτινες εὐνούχισαν
ἑαυτοὺς διὰ τὴν βασιλείαν τῶν οὐρανῶν

(Matt. 19:12)

You might pray to God to give you some insight into the meaning of that Scripture verse, but chances are nothing will happen unless you know Greek. Yet if you insist on eavesdropping on that first-century group of people because, for some reason or other, you believe that what they listen to in their first-century world is of some importance to you, then your first requirement would be to find a translator so that you might find out what is being said. Bible translations serve this purpose.

But what do such Bible translations offer you? At most they let you, a foreigner, get to know what those first-century Greek-speaking folks are saying. But what someone says and what he means to say are often quite distinct. Should you tell your girlfriend that you love the gold of her hair, do you mean that her hair will make an excellent hedge against inflation? And why would you want a hedge against inflation rather than a fence, a wall, or a stand of trees? The words we use to say and speak do in fact embody meaning, but the meaning does not come from the words. Meaning derives

1

from the general social system of the speakers of a language. This is why what one says and what one means to say can often be quite different, especially for persons not sharing the same social system. By translating the Gospel of Matthew into English, what we do is transplant our first-century Syrian Hellenists into our modes of saying, and all too often we presuppose that what they say embodies our modes of meaning as well. An English translation of Matthew 19:12 yields the following:

> For there are eunuchs who have been so from birth,
> and there are eunuchs who have been made eunuchs by men,
> and there are eunuchs who have made themselves eunuchs
> for the sake of the kingdom of heaven.

This is the English equivalent of what you would have heard as you eavesdropped on the Christian group reading Matthew in the scene above. When you heard it in Greek in first-century Syria, you were the foreigner observing and overhearing a group of natives. But when you read your Bible translation in your twentieth-century surroundings, you transfer the coherent words of first-century non-Westerners, say, into your own social world. You are in fact hearing the words of a transplanted group of foreigners from another time and place, with you, the native, wondering what in the world these people are talking about. Why the mention of eunuchs at all? Eunuchs are hardly the topic of our dinner-time conversations, much less the object of prolonged sermonizing in our churches. And why the peculiar listing of three types of eunuchs? While we employ all sorts of verbal listings, do we have any such three-type listings that we habitually use in our conversations?

Perhaps the first and largest step that someone in twentieth-century Western English-speaking society can take toward understanding the Bible is to realize that when we read the Bible we are listening to the words of a transplanted group of foreigners. It takes only the ability to read to find out what these foreigners are saying, but it takes far more to find out what they mean. If meaning derives from a social system, while wording (e.g., speaking or writing) simply embodies meanings from the social system, then any adequate understanding of the Bible requires some understanding of the social system embodied in the words that make up our sacred Scripture. That the author of Matthew's Gospel speaks of eunuchs, for example, can be easily verified. That the word "eunuch" refers to a castrated male can also be easily verified. But why the reference to a castrated male? What does being called a eunuch mean to a first-century Palestinian male? What does it mean in terms of male social roles and values? How can a person in twentieth-century Western society find out such information relative to the first-century Mediterranean world? The purpose of this book is to explain how we might retrieve such information as well as to set out some examples of such information and its utility for getting to understand the Bible.

Questions about the social norms and values that made up the world of first-century Palestine, as well as methods for answering such questions, are rather new in biblical studies. Such questions and methods are the contemporary end product of a whole series of useful approaches to understanding the Bible. They have developed largely because they are the logical outcome of attempts to understand the Word of God in our own day and age.

At bottom, biblical scholarship from antiquity to the present (e.g., read St. Augustine, *On Christian Doctrine*) presupposes that studying the Bible for the purpose of gaining some understanding is much like eavesdropping on a transplanted group of foreigners with the purpose of getting to understand them. Hence scholars have provided reliable translations to help people find out what those foreigners are saying. If the Bible is important to us, we would want to know where these foreigners come from so that we might relate what they are saying to some concrete objects, objects of the sort found in their world. We would want to know about the persons they make reference to as they speak, about when they lived, about what they did and built. Scholars have produced biblical encyclopedias to provide this sort of information. We might also want to situate the country of origin of these foreigners in terms of geographical space and environment. The various biblical atlases help us do this.

If we look through our Bible translations, encyclopedias, and atlases, we will find information about who our foreigners are, what they say, and where they come from—but all from the viewpoint of our twentieth-century Western existence. All this information makes it more than apparent that they are indeed foreigners, not from our country and not from our social group at all. Is this amount of information sufficient for you to say that you can understand what they say and mean to say as you read their words in the Bible? Or is it just about enough information to help you situate them relative to yourself and to place them relative to other foreign groups?

Chances are that if other people knew only your name, your social rank, some of your statements, and some geographical information about you, you would say that they really cannot understand you yet. What more would they have to know? What more would you have to know to understand a foreigner? Just as you get to know yourself by comparison with others, by comparing how you are similar to and different from others, how you are just like others and unique relative to others, so you might now move on to asking the same questions about our hypothetical group of foreigners. How are they similar to others in their area of the world and period of history; how are they different? How are they just like other people in their time and place; how are they unique relative to others? How did they dissociate themselves from other larger groups to form distinct, separate groups with somewhat shared yet unique histories? Scholarly histories of the Bible present this sort of information. Now is this sort of information sufficient for you to say that you can understand our group of foreigners? Would you think others might get to understand you sufficiently if they knew who your ancestors were and where they came from; what they did and how that affected their movements; how they variously intermarried in terms of your family tree, how your parents decided to marry; how you grew up from childhood to adolescence? While these *how* questions take us a few steps beyond the what, who, when, and where questions that we began with, do they suffice to generate any sort of full understanding? If your information is still insufficient, let us try another tack.

Suppose I listened very carefully to everything you say. I could then catalogue your speech patterns and relate them to various contexts of your life. I could learn the patterns you use to tell a joke, to threaten your friends and acquaintances, to flatter your parents, to cajole a person of the opposite sex, to pray to God or your friends or the tax man, to greet a teacher or an equal. My catalog would consist of the different forms or patterns of speech that you use for different purposes in different social contexts. When such forms or patterns of speech get written down, we can call them literary forms or literary patterns. Normally there is a relationship between the literary and speech form you might use and the social context in which you find yourself. You can find hundreds of such patterns of writing—which you really know very well, although you probably do not know you know them so well—in newspapers. You know that a food ad is different from a movie ad, so you won't look up the food ads to find out what is playing at the local cinema. You know the society-page form of wedding announcement and social event description, and how they differ from the social questions submitted to Ann Landers, and how these differ from the medical advice column. You also know how all of the above differ from the literary form of an obituary, an editorial, letters to the editor, a national news story, local news story, and, that most important of pages, the sports page, with its endless literary forms for football, baseball, basketball, hockey, track and field, and the like. Now suppose I can also catalog the speech and writing forms of our hypothetical group of foreigners. Will that help me understand them sufficiently? From such literary study, I can tell you what they are saying, the English equivalents of their words, and how they put their sentences together to express threat, fear, greeting, birth announcements, arguments, teaching, jokes, consolation, law, encouragement, and the like. I can likewise tell you how they construct their oral or written paragraphs into prose and poetry, into history and legend, into letters and speeches.

For example, consider the eunuch passage cited above from Matthew

19:12. I can tell you quite a bit about it by comparing it with other similar literary forms in the Bible. It has the basic pattern of a numbered parable like we find in the book of Proverbs (the Hebrew word for proverb and parable is identical, *mashal*). For starters, look at Proverbs 30:33:

> For pressing milk produces curds,
>> pressing the nose produces blood,
>> and pressing anger produces strife.

The way such literary patterns work is that the first and second (and more) elements are concrete, imaginable, pictures, while the last item of the series is abstract, moral, dealing with some hidden dimension of human behavior. The first two (or more) elements set the stage for understanding the final element. In the above parable, how does churning milk and hitting a person in the nose set the stage for understanding the final element?

This pattern is clear in the explicitly numbered parables, e.g., Proverbs 30:18–19:

> Three things are too wonderful for me;
>> four I do not understand:
> the way of an eagle in the sky,
>> the way of a serpent on a rock,
> the way of a ship on the high seas,
>> and the way of a man with a maiden.

The question to ask here is how do the common features of the concrete pictures—a flying eagle, a slithering serpent on a rock, and a ship on the sea—set the stage for the final point? What do the eagle, the serpent, and the ship in question have in common? You might note that none of them leaves a trace once they have gone by. How does this insight set the stage for understanding the final point, which is abstract, moral, dealing with a hidden dimension of human behavior?

In a parable, something other and something else gets pointed out by the concrete picture, and it is up to the hearer to figure out the something other and something else. This is typical of "devious" Oriental wisdom, which likewise abounds in the parables of Jesus. There are other such numbered parables attributed to Jesus in Matthew. For example, Matthew 8:20:

> Foxes have holes,
>> and birds of the air have nests;
> but the Son of man has nowhere to lay his head.

Or Matthew 10:41–42:

> He who receives a prophet because he is a prophet shall receive a prophet's reward,

> and he who receives a righteous man because he is a righteous man
> shall receive a righteous man's reward.
> And whoever gives to one of these little ones even a cup of cold water
> because he is a disciple, truly, I say to you, he shall not lose his
> reward.

Or Matthew 11:7-9:

> What did you go out into the wilderness to behold?
> A reed shaken by the wind?
> Why then did you go out?
> To see a man clothed in soft raiment? . . .
> Why then did you go out?
> To see a prophet?
> Yes, I tell you, and more than a prophet.

Thus the literary pattern of our eunuch passage is that of a numbered parable
in which the first two (or more) elements offer concrete pictures that set the stage
for understanding the final element, which is the main point of the passage.

Relative to the Bible, modern biblical commentaries will furnish you
with this sort of literary analysis along with the what, when, where, and
historical how mentioned above. This sort of literary analysis, the study of
writing patterns or literary forms, is another dimension of the what and how
question we might put to the people in our texts in order to get to understand
them. Again, if you were to have all of the information singled out so far,
would you have enough to understand our hypothetical group of foreigners
sufficiently? If people had all this sort of information about you, would that
be enough for them to say that they know you just about as well as they can?

So far one sort of question has been left out of the picture, although it
constantly lurks behind all of the who, what, when, where, and how
questions we might put to our hypothetical foreigners. This question, of
course, is the why question. In the eunuch passage, why precisely is there the
mention of eunuchs? What meaning does the value embodied in the social
role of eunuch bear, and why does it bear that meaning in that particular
social system? The specific details needed to answer these questions will be
spelled out in chapter 2, below. But in order to set out those details in a
meaningful way, as well as in order to evaluate them adequately, a number
of presuppositions of a rather abstract sort have to be set out so that you
might better understand the perspectives of this book. These presuppositions deal with the meaning and dimensions of cross-cultural knowledge, of
why questions and their answers, with regard both to ourselves and to those
who people the pages of the Bible. You can very well skip the remainder of
this chapter and move on to the rest of the book without appreciable damage
to the book's contents. But if in the subsequent chapters you begin to
wonder how any author can make the claims set forth relative to people so

much removed from us in time and place, you would do well to study through the rest of this chapter.

The Presuppositions Behind This Book

Knowledge about others as well as about ourselves might be conveniently divided into three types: (1) awareness knowledge or that-knowledge: information about something or someone, that something or someone does or does not exist (what/who), its/his/her location in space (where) or time (when); (2) usable knowledge or how-to and how-knowledge: information necessary to use something or interact with someone properly or to understand how uses and interactions are generated (how); (3) principle knowledge or why-knowledge: information about the cultural scripts and cues, about the cultural models behind the applicable facts, along with the required faith in or commitment to the presuppositions and assumptions that make the cultural scripts, cues, and models evident. If all this sounds a bit abstract, consider what sort of knowledge is needed to invent, develop, maintain, and operate a television set. Why-knowledge, the knowledge of principles, is about the big picture, about the meaning of it all, about the implied values and meanings that ultimately explain behavior. For example, if someone were to attempt to understand you sufficiently, along with the who, what, when, where, and how of your life, that someone would need to understand the why of your life, your standpoint or horizon. To understand your standpoint or horizon, that someone would have to know your experiences, how you imagined those experiences, what sort of insights helped you make sense of those experiences in terms of societal and familial expectations, how you learned to think about those insights in terms of socially available models of meaning, what sort of effect those models of meaning had on you and those important to you, and, finally, how you acted, what you did about it, and how such action led to new experiences, images, insights, models, criticism, and more action, and so on.

Nature, Culture, Person

If you examine your life, you will see that you have occupied a number of standpoints and lived life from a number of horizons. The succession of standpoints and horizons of your life make up your personal story thus far. If someone had the information that went into the making of your story, he or she would be able to grasp the meaning of it all, the why of your life so far, On what basis would that person get to understand you? I would suggest that the sort of understanding I am speaking of is based on a presupposition in our own culture that might be articulated as follows: *All human beings are entirely the same, entirely different, and somewhat the same and somewhat different at the same time* (see Figure 1).

Figure 1. *The Basic Presupposition—Nature, Culture, Person*

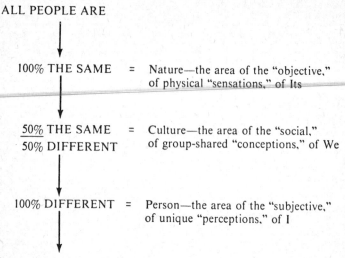

ALL PEOPLE ARE

100% THE SAME   =   Nature—the area of the "objective,"
                               of physical "sensations," of Its

50% THE SAME   =   Culture—the area of the "social,"
50% DIFFERENT   of group-shared "conceptions," of We

100% DIFFERENT =   Person—the area of the "subjective,"
                               of unique "perceptions," of I

AT THE SAME TIME, SIMULTANEOUSLY, CONCURRENTLY

From this point of view, human beings are individualized or personalized representatives of human nature immersed in particular cultures. It also means that all human knowing is simultaneously objective, subjective, and social.

The first part of the presupposition, *all human beings are entirely the same,* focuses our attention on similarities. Who posed for the picture of the human heart in an anatomy textbook? Does it matter? Focus upon recurrent similarity produces the area we call "nature," that is, all that exists apart from purposeful, willful human influence. We also call this area "the objective," and ascribe it to the "sciences." Nature is said to subsist in regular, patterned forms that make up our physical environments. Within this perspective, scientists are said to "discover" patterns of similarity called "laws," and so long as they prescind from willful, human influence, their enterprise is said to be "objective."

The second part of the presupposition, *all human beings are entirely different,* focuses our attention upon the uniqueness of individual human beings. Of whom can you use the word "I" with meaning? Focus upon uniqueness produces what we call "personhood." This is the area of personal story, of incommunicable biography. Persons are said to develop and live out their stories in unique fashion, a fashion said to be "subjective."

The third part of the presupposition, *all human beings are somewhat the same and somewhat different,* focuses our attention on the interplay of similarities and differences within human communities. To what does the word "we" refer? If you and I are truly unique and therefore incommunicable in our uniqueness, how do we communicate at all? We communicate on a "we" basis. Focus upon this interplay of partial similarity and difference produces the area called "culture." Culture is an organized system of symbols by which persons, things, and events are endowed with rather specific and socially shared meanings and values. Cultures are said to "create" patterns of shared meaning and feeling which combine to shape the social world of a given group. Humanists, as opposed to scientists, attempt to "articulate" such patterns of shared symbolic meaning, and, more often than not, the outcomes of their enterprise are said to be "creative interpretations," or "learned opinions." Their enterprise is said to be "social."

I should like to insist that the presupposition under scrutiny conclude with the phrase *at the same time.* While scientists study human sensations, cultures create human conceptions, and individuals generate personal perceptions, yet human knowing is, in fact, simultaneously objective, subjective, and social. Nature, culture, and person tend to kaleidoscope, with all simultaneously present, yet with emphasis on the one or the other, depending on various factors. What I mean is that to understand your story adequately, I need to know not only the who, what, when, where, and how of your physical and psychological human nature and unique personhood, but also the why's and wherefore's of our commonly shared cultural story that fill the who, what, when, where, and how with mutually appreciable meaning and value.

To return to our transplanted group of foreigners, in our case the New Testament writings, our eavesdropping with the purpose of understanding them can generate understanding only if we pay careful attention to the cultural system that "created" them and which they embody. In terms of nature, the persons described in the New Testament would be just like us and everyone else in the world. In terms of personhood and uniqueness, they would be as unfathomable as we are to each other. On the other hand, in terms of cultural story, cultural cues, cultural script, they would be somewhat like us, yet somewhat unlike us: like us in terms of human nature; unlike us in terms of the cultural interpretation of human nature.

Consider what we have so far relative to understanding the New Testament writings. What we have is a group of first-century A.D. (when) Hellenistic writings, written in Greek, for the most part by Jews deriving from the easternmost shores of the Mediterranean (what, who, where), in an area where Aramaic and Hebrew were the usual languages. Yet the area was part of the Roman Empire, throughout which the common language was

Greek. Bible translations offer English equivalents of what the authors of the writings have to say. To aid our imagination, atlases and encyclopedias offer information about the concrete environment, artifacts, significant individuals and groups mentioned directly or indirectly in the texts. Histories explain how events prior to the New Testament period came to influence the situation in which the Jesus movement began, how the Christian movement got under way and initially developed, and the like. Commentaries on the individual New Testament writings point out the meanings of words and the literary forms of individual books (Gospels, history, letters, tracts, "apocalypse") as well as of specific passages within given writings (parables, proverbs, genealogies, birth announcements, psalms, conflict discussions, miracle stories, recommendations, travel plans, and the like). Biblical commentators often focus on the meaning of a literary form or the meaning of words in that culture, while historians talk about the meaning of behavior. The question of meaning is a *why* question. On what basis can a why question be adequately answered? On what basis can a why question in your life, in your group's behavior, be adequately answered? I submit that such why questions can only be answered in terms of cultural story. If commentators, historians, and ordinary Bible readers derive meaning from the New Testament, the question we might put to them is whether such meaning comes from *their* cultural story or the cultural story of the people who produced the texts. Were I to interpret all your actions in terms of my own behavior, I am afraid you might end up socking me in the mouth. After all, where I come from, all who "carry out" groceries from a supermarket pride themselves on their shoplifting abilities, and I would presume the same for you and everyone else. You might find this very offensive. Yet when it comes to deriving meaning from the Bible, there is no one to give you pause, to urge you to reconsider, to sock you in the mouth in case of misinterpretation.

The misinterpretation I am referring to comes from identifying your cultural story with human nature: "Since we do it this way, all people of all times must do it this way." This is an "Archie Bunkerism," known in learned circles as ethnocentrism. When applied to history, it is called anachronism—imposing the cultural artifacts and behavior of your own period on people of the past. Ethnocentric anachronisms are cute on the lips of children, readily discernible when it comes to concrete things, e.g. the Holy Family taking a TWA flight on the flight to Egypt; Paul buying a King James Version of the Bible to quote when he preached; or Jesus traveling from Nazareth to Jerusalem in a jeep. But such ethnocentric anachronisms are insidiously irretrievable when it comes to the meaning of behavior. For example, Jesus condemned divorce, people in our society get divorced, so Jesus must be condemning that sort of behavior in our society. The problem is: do marriage and divorce mean the same thing when Jesus speaks of them and when we speak of them?

Understanding Culture

The only way to avoid such misinterpretations, such "Archie Bunkerisms," such ethnocentric anachronisms, is to understand the culture from which our foreign writings come as well as to understand our own cultural story along with realizing that perhaps in most instances the cultural stories are very different. In this way we might get to understand those foreigners as we eavesdrop on what they said to each other and as we attempt to imagine the behavior they allude to. What then does culture mean, and how do we come to understand a culture?

What the term "culture" means in this book is what cultural or social anthropologists mean when they use the term. For example, Clyde Kluckhohn describes culture as follows:

> Culture consists of patterns, explicit and implicit, of and for behavior acquired and transmitted by symbols, constituting the distinctive achievement of human groups, including their embodiments in artifacts: the essential core of culture consists of traditional (i.e., historically derived and selected) ideas and especially their attached values; culture systems may, on the one hand, be considered as products of action, on the other as conditioning influences upon further action.

What this means is that culture is a system of symbols relating to and embracing people, things, and events that are socially symboled. Symboling means filling people, things, and events with meaning and value (feeling), making them meaningful in such a way that all the members of a given group mutually share, appreciate, and live out of that meaning and value in some way. For example, on the level of nature, human beings mate and reproduce because males of the species fertilize the ova of females of the species. When the fertilized ovum comes to term, the female drops the offspring. What culture does is take this process and the agents in the process and fill them with meaning and value. The sperm contributor is interpreted as "father," the ovum bearer as "mother," and the offspring as "child." I am sure you do not celebrate Ovum Bearer's Day, even if you are terribly scientifically minded. Nor do you view the sperm contributor who hangs around the ovum bearer of your existence as the family sperm bank. Rather, you relate to these beings as parents (a cultural interpretation of their role and activity). Together with them, you form a family (a cultural interpretation of the naturing and nurturing group). You learn to interpret their relationship to each other and to you as affection and loyalty (a cultural interpretation of this inner group relation or event).

What culture does is take what is available in the physical and human environment and interpret it, fill it with meaning and feeling. In this perspective we are somewhat like and somewhat unlike the rest of mankind. We are like them, naturally, insofar as all peoples (as far as we know) mate, reproduce, live in some variation of a cave (house), get around (transportation), and the like. We differ from them culturally insofar as different groups of people assign different meanings and values to being a father or mother, male or female, having children, and to types of housing, modes of transportation, and so on. A child may be viewed as an economic asset or an economic liability. All houses are not constructed equal; there are high-class and low-class houses. Transportation for an Eskimo is not the same as transportation for an American, and a 1971 Pinto does not mean the same thing as a 1980 Porsche. Culture is all about shared meanings and feelings.

Language is a most important aspect and perhaps the best example of culture. As a natural phenomenon, language is speech, airwaves that are patterned in a socially appreciable way as the air passes from the lungs through the vocal chords over tongue, teeth, and through the mouth cavity. You can sense speech when these airwaves hit the tympanum of your ear and register some impression in your brain. Culture fills these naturally and personally produced air waves with meaning and feeling by patterning them in socially appreciable ways. Thus more than one person share the same patterns, allowing for communication on a "we" level—the "we" being all of us who share the same patterns of meaning and feeling. When you do not share speech patterns, you simply do not understand a language. When you do not share behavior patterns, you simply do not understand what another person is doing. Should you identify your language (culture) with human being (nature), you would tend to think that all people should speak Human (English), just as you do; if they do not, they are either subhuman or non-human. This is ethnocentrism again. The same holds for behavior (and language is a form of behavior). Should you identify your forms and patterns of behavior (culture) with human being (nature), you would tend to think that all human beings should behave according to the patterns or norms of your group; if they do not, they are either subhuman or non-human.

The Bigger Picture—Cultural Cues

In order to avoid the pitfalls to understanding posed by ethnocentrism, it would be useful to try to get the bigger picture into which any given thought, utterance, or action normally fits. This is the overall system of the culture, the so-called cultural matrix or cultural script. What I mean might be illustrated as follows. When we claim to understand a person's hostile behavior on a given occasion, we mean that we consider it as a part of a more complete pattern of behavior, a larger frame, which characterizes this person or people in general in a given culture. On the other hand, when a particular mode of behavior does not seem to follow a pattern that we know, and we cannot place it in a larger frame comprehensible to us, we usually claim not to understand the behavior. When we understand a word, we mean that we know how it can be used in context with other words, a larger frame. We understand what bone, leg, finger, or head signify in their relation to the larger structure of which they are parts. In our culture, the fall of an apple is understood only in the larger frame of gravity. These examples (can you add others?) indicate that human understanding is *relative,* i.e., each item we understand derives its culturally adequate meaning from something else, the larger frame, to which it is related and in which it seems to fit.

This might lead you to ask, "Where does it stop?" It stops when we cannot find a frame or larger pattern for the idea, person, or event which we wish to understand. This in fact is the normal experience of a person in a new and unrelated culture, observing strange and unusual (in the sense of not usual) behavior for the first time. In such a situation a person finds no frame for the behavior he or she wishes to understand. "Culture shock" is an accumulation of such experiences that overwhelms a person. A similar sort of "culture shock" is the normal experience of a person faced with new real-life information or real-life problems that no longer fit the ultimate larger frame that he previously used to understand and cope with such information or such problems in the past, for example the larger frame symboled with the word "God." Many persons question the existence of God simply because they outgrow their symbol of the ultimate "really Real" that served them so well in childhood and early adolescence. Their symbol for the ultimate larger frame no longer serves as an adequate frame for the new realities they wish to understand. Moving on to more adequate larger frames, both in cross-cultural understanding and in religious experience within one's culture, is a sort of "conversion" experience. But conversion from what to what? Where did you begin to learn and be grabbed by the meanings and values that you personify?

Was your first difficult decision in life choosing what language to speak as you emerged from your mother's womb? Did you have to take time out of your busy play schedule as an infant to decide whether you would behave as a boy or a girl? How did you ultimately decide that "nanee, nanee, poopoo" was a terrible thing to say to a fellow three-year-old? All these aspects of culture are assimilated by a process called enculturation. They are assimilated in such a way that most people do not even realize the extent to which their culture's values and meanings, ideas and feelings, determine what is really real for them. The patterns of culture become a sort of second nature, helping all in our group to make sense of experience, interact with each other and our environment with meaning and satisfaction, and giving us the certainty that particular persons, things, and events make no sense, lack meaning and are thoroughly dissatisfying.

In short, we assimilate the meanings and values of our culture much as we have assimilated our shared language. All cultural symbols, from simple ones like offering a poor person a hand-out to complex ones like marriage and kinship, are patterned, follow rules and norms, just like language. And just as many people speak English quite well yet do not know any grammar (the patterns or rules of the language), so many people carry on quite well in our culture without any knowledge of the patterns and norms underlying their behavior. But whether explicit or implicit, there certainly are patterns and rules underlying behavior. Just as, even without knowledge of grammar, you know a foreigner when you hear one, so also without knowledge of cultural norms, you know male and female behavior when you see it.

Just what sort of cultural norms go to make up the essential core of a given culture? In other words, what sort of cultural cues did we assimilate from those significant others who reared us to live in a meaningful way in our society? We might conveniently differentiate six classes of such cultural cues:

1) *Perception:* those cues defining in what ways and how any person, thing, or event is to be perceived, the meaning they are said to bear relative to me and others. These cues of perception make up the central, large frames of reference in the culture. They include the cognitive orientation of the culture, like perceptions that all goods in life are limitless, that every effect has an adequate cause, that morally good persons win out in the end, that lawful competition leads to achievement. To see how these work, consider what you would do if your car broke down or if the light in your room went out. First of all, do you ascribe the breakdown to some person (the people on the GM assembly line who made you a lemon) or to some thing (faulty sparkplugs)? Do you try to remedy the situation by recourse to significant people by praying to them, or do you check the immediate adequate cause, e.g., light bulb, switch, fuse box, etc.? Your behavior would flow from implicit norms of perception shared by all of us in this culture. If it did not, you would be judged as slightly off your rocker, not all there, harmless but crazy, and the like.

2) *Feeling:* those cues telling us what and how we must feel in a given situation. For example, should you see a person doing 60 in a 25-mile zone on a motorcycle, then watch him proceed to slam into a pole, should you laugh or look serious? If you move over toward him, are you to sit back and feel superior or move in and offer help? Who is to behave how, with what

feeling, at a funeral? Do males and females alike cry, or is the macho male to look impassive, while the females can give free vent to their feelings in tears and wailing? How is one to feel at a football game, the wedding of a friend, upon the purchase of a new car? We had to learn how to feel in specific situations.

3) *Acting:* those cues telling us what we must do or avoid doing both in general and in specific occasions. For example, who is supposed to invite whom on a date, the male or the female? How should a male walk and hold his hands and head? How should a female walk and hold her hands and head? What if a male normally wiggles his hips as he walks? What are male gestures, female gestures? What is the proper behavior in an embarrassing situation, fight or flight? What should you do to someone picking on you unjustly, be it a bully or the tax man? And what if they pick on you justly? Again, we all learned such sorts of cues for acting.

4) *Believing:* those cues telling us what we must believe in and profess. We believe in those persons, things, and events about which we think we should be unashamedly intolerant should they be called in question, mocked, or ridiculed. To find your beliefs-in, think of what you would rather fearlessly stand up for: your parents, brothers, and sisters; the American flag when mocked by a foreigner; going to college to get ahead in the world or just because learning is good in itself; being treated as an individual number or as an individual person; holding good ideals or holding no ideals; having practical know-how or just book knowledge; being good in sports or in dating, or just knowing about sports and dating. We, too, learned our beliefs-in.

5) *Admiring:* those cues telling us what and whom we must hold in awe, what and whom we ought to admire and respect. For example, what sorts of persons do your parents tell you they wish you were like? What sorts of persons do you want to be like? What kind of person is the most popular date on the college campus? What is your preference in a "good-looking" male or female? Who do you think embodies what you stand for: Cliff Richard, Elaine Page, Billy Graham, Stevie Wonder? The cues for admiring which you have learned will tell you.

6) *Striving:* those cues telling us what are worthwhile goals in life, with the significant others legitimating our selection. For example, who tells you that the way you dress is proper: parents, peers, friends? What sort of success do you look for in life: money, sex, family, power over others, publicity? The cues for striving we have learned set out the culturally available goals.

Now just as we learned and assimilated language in the process of being enculturated, so too we have learned and assimilated sets of cultural cues that lead us to perceive, feel, act, believe, admire, and strive in a way that makes sense to ourselves and others in our society. What these cues do for us is to generate meaningful behavior, behavior that is patterned and endowed with feeling, with emotion. They generate valuable behavior, behavior that is valued and makes sense within a range of meanings and feelings. The reason for my going over the meaning of culture and cultural cues in this context is to call your attention to the fact that it is extremely likely that our group of foreigners, our New Testament writings, come from people who were likewise enculturated into cues of perception, feeling, acting, believing, admiring, and striving. Jesus, the Gospel authors, and the persons referred to in their writings, Paul, the Pharisees, Sadducees, Zealots, the early Christian community—all these persons derived from and lived according to the patterns of their societies. Their behavior made sense; their interactions took place according to the patterns of their culture; their values were judged noble or ignoble in line with the cues shared in the groups of the time. When they got angry at each other, they knew why. For the believing Christian, the Incarnation of the Word of God means the enculturation of God's Word. And the only way the Word of God, both in the New Testament writings and in the person of Jesus, can make sense to us today is by studying it within the larger frame of first-century A.D. Palestinian and Mediterranean culture. For along with learning the who, what, when, where, and how of the New Testament, the study of the culture of the period will offer insight into the why's of the behavior pictured in our texts.

Why the Bigger Picture—Man the Model-Maker

How then do we get to understand another culture? How do you get to understand anything? Understanding seems to lie in the genetic ability of most human beings (after puberty) to think abstractly. Abstract thinking, often called generalization or generalized reasoning, is the ability to think in terms of ideas or concepts instead of concrete images. Ideas and concepts are abstract representations of the essences of things; they are the result of the ability to "chunk" common qualities from a large number of concretely different items, and then to express these chunks in terms of non-concrete signs and symbols. For example, instead of imagining (or talking about) an individual Jonathan apple or Bartlett pear or cooking banana or Melba peach or Italian plum or navel orange or Hawaian pineapple, we can form the idea or concept of fruit. Now what the word "fruit" refers to is an idea of what all the previous list have in common, their similarities. And this common or similar element of "fruitness" really has no concrete, physical existence at all; it is really not concrete at all. Obviously, what concretely exists are actual and specific apples, pears, bananas, and the like. This is a sort of first-level abstraction or chunk, for we can go further. We can take such abstractions as fruit, meat, vegetables, bread, and the like and produce a still higher abstraction, in this case "food." Every higher abstraction is a sort of bigger picture. Moreover, along with generating such abstractions, we also have the ability to make relationships among or between abstractions. We can say, for example, food is necessary for human life. And even beyond this, we can take statements of relationships and put them in sequences called syllogistic reasoning; we can make deductions from general abstract principles to concrete cases, and inductions from concrete cases to general abstract principles; we can analyze by taking abstractions apart into lower-level abstractions to the concrete level; and we can synthesize by putting chunks together to ever higher levels of abstraction.

Why do human beings think abstractly? Perhaps the main reason, as the experimental psychologists tell us, is that human beings are unable to keep any more than seven (plus or minus two) disparate elements in mental focus at one time. What abstraction enables us to do is to represent and make some order among the countless experiences we undergo in the course of our interacting with our multiple environments. In short, our ability to think abstractly enable us to generate some orderly or patterned understanding of our complex experiences. The word "culture" that we have described previously is such an abstraction.

Now patterns of abstract thought, patterns of relationships among abstractions, are called models (or theories, or when very high-level abstractions, paradigms). Models are asbtract, simplified representations of more complex real world objects and interactions. Like abstract thought, the purpose of models is to enable and facilitate understanding. Understanding, then, is the result of the process of abstraction in terms of patterns which order, classify, and give shape to human experiences. What is adequate understanding? As I just mentioned, models are generalizations or abstract descriptions of real world experiences; they are approximate, simple representations of more complex forms, processes, and functions of physical and non-physical phenomena. Now because models are simplifications, they are notorious for misfitting the real world experiences they attempt to represent. To reduce the misfit as much as possible, our cultural tradition—both scientific and humanistic—espouses a validation process presently called "the scientific method." The scientific method consists of the following steps: (1) postulate a model (or theory or paradigm); (2) test the model against the real world experience it relates to; (3) modify the model in terms of the outcome of the test to reduce the misfit by detecting errors of omission or commission. This method serves as a safeguard against the twin pitfalls of human understanding: superificiality and inaccuracy. Because models cannot be proved—after all they are postulated, i.e., they derive from a sort of insight that seems to hold experiences together in such a way as to make sense—they can only be validated. What validation means is that the generalizations or abstract statements deriving from the model have been checked out according to the steps of the scientific method and have been found adequate, given the experiences or data the model is meant to chunk. In other words, all the data readily fit the postulated model, and anyone can check it out.

Now understanding cultures is possible because of our ability to think abstractly, to make models of experience, and to compare the various models we come up with. Model-making or abstract thinking points to how we can understand a culture other than our own as well as our own. But why can we claim to attempt the understanding of an alien culture like that of the persons who people the New Testament? Our own culture outfits us with two important cues of perception that work to this end. The first is the awareness of the possibility that we ourselves can change, that there are many roles open to us, that people in history and in our own milieu have taken on roles other than the ones we have. The second cue is the ability to take on the role of another empathetically, to move into someone else's shoes, to perceive from someone else's horizon or standpoint. (Sympathy is your putting them in your place, like when you feel sympathy for a dog that hurt its paw.) Empathy leads to an awareness of the actual differences and potential similarities between another and yourself, between another group and your own group.

Models in Cultural Anthropology

So what we need in order to understand our hypothetical group of foreigners—the New Testament writings and the behavior of the people portrayed in them—are some adequate models that would enable us to understand cross-culturally, that would force us to keep our meanings and values out of their behavior, so that we might understand them on their own terms. If you will recall, the purpose of models is to generate understanding. Models formulate relationships among the persons, things, and events that we want to study. These relationships between various persons and groups, persons and things, as well as the interactions and activities such persons and groups undertake—all these have to be named and described. For example, the ovum bearer of your existence gets named "mother"; mothers do not exist except in terms of children, so mother presupposes child, and child presupposes mother. What is the normal behavior of mother toward child? This interaction might be called "nurturing," and we might generalize by saying that in our society mothers nurture their children. So big deal! But why the mother-child interaction? What does it mean relative to the social group in general? What does it mean relative to social roles, role playing, role taking, and role making within a given culture?

Models in anthropology at a rather high level of abstraction derive from certain presuppositions, much like models in chemistry, physics, and biology. These presuppositions that underpin the models revolve around the nature of groups or social systems. The first question about the mother-child interaction that I posed above (What does this interaction mean relative to the social group in general?) presupposes that a social system is a group of interacting persons whose interaction is structured (patterned behavior, structure) and oriented around common concerns or purposes (functions). In other words, meaningful human behavior is behavior according to socially shared patterns (remember the cultural cues above) performed for socially meaningful purposes (functions). If we were to take a still photograph of our entire society, freeze all activity for a moment, so to say, and then analyze what is going on in terms of what relationships and for what purposes, we would end up with a general image of the main outine of the structures of the society along with their functions. This sort of still picture, when verbalized as social theory or model, is called *structural functionalism*. The still picture that we get to see is one of a society that is cohesive and integrated by consensus on meanings, values, and norms. The various smaller social systems like family, government, economics, education, and religion are bound together by common values and norms, and these smaller social systems (called social institutions) interact with each other in a cooperative and harmonious way. Thus society is in equilibrium, in good balance, and the social system tends to persist with minor amounts of adaptive change. Changes in one institution lead to changes in others, so if you wanted to start a revolution, you could do so by changing any one of the smaller social systems.

The structural functionalist model presupposes that every society is a relatively persistent, stable structure of elements. Every society is a well-integrated structure of elements. Every element in a society has a function; it renders a contribution to maintaining society as a whole system. Every functioning social structure is based on a consensus of values among its members. In this still-photo type of model, any social change is deviance; the picture is static.

Now still-life photographs, much like those taken by reconnaissance planes, are very useful in helping to understand what was going on when the picture was taken. So one good way to get to understand our group of foreigners is to find out what sort of structures or patterns of behavior were typical in their society, what norms expressed the "oughts" for this sort of behavior, and how such behavior supported and fulfilled a useful social function.

Structural functionalism pictures social systems as the result of consensus, a sort of consensual obligation in which people freely choose to oblige themselves in a certain way. But this is obviously not the whole picture. As with human behavior in general, so too social systems reveal freedom as well as constraints. You are free to leave your classroom, but you are forced or constrained to use a door or window to do so. You are not free to walk through the walls except by using a door or window. Socially, you are free to date and marry anyone in the whole world. But you are constrained, held back, from actually doing so by your own limited physical, psychological, and social existence. You can't meet everyone in the world in a lifetime; you can't be everywhere at once; you do not have access to all social groups and classes, and so on. I mention freedom and constraint because, while the structural functionalist model emphasizes consensus or freedom in the formation and endurance of social systems (the still-life photo approach), the flip-side theory would emphasize the constraints human groups put on each other. This flip-side theory is called the *conflict model* (also known as coercion, power or interest models or theories).

The conflict theory is more like a slow-motion film. It would have us imagine social systems as consisting of various groups (e.g., family, government, economics, education, religion) which have differing goals and interests and therefore use coercive tactics on each other in order to realize their own goals. Each of the various groups protects the distinctive interest of its members, and relations between various groups include disagreement, strain, conflict, and force—as well as consensus and cooperation. If dissent and conflict are part of the normal social process, then any social system must also protect and assert its members' interests in relations with other systems, even by challenging the established order. No system can survive if it fails to maintain a favorable balance between its members' personal needs and the demands of the broader society. Thus the mother-father-child set of norms (the family) must function to protect and develop its members so that they may achieve their goals and assert their interests within a societal context of conflict.

The conflict model presupposes that all units of social organization, i.e., persons and groups in a society, are continuously changing unless some force intervenes to correct this change. Change is all around us, ubiquitous. Wherever there is social life, there is conflict. What holds social systems and their sub-systems together is not consensus, but constraint, the coercion of some by others, not universal agreement. While value systems can generate change, constraint generates conflict. Conflict is all around us because constraint is all around us wherever human beings set up social organizations.

From this perspective and in terms of this sort of model, a good way to understand our group of foreigners is to find out what elements or factors interfere in the normal process of change. Absence of conflict would be surprising and abnormal. What sorts of conflict typify the behavior depicted in the New Testament? In this slow-motion film type of model, there is an unending process of change in society—as in the individual human being. Social change, deviance, is normal. Social pressures toward obligatory consent (like in your peer group) lead to reactions that result in changes of various sorts.

As I mentioned previously, human beings work up models in order to understand their experiences. No model that we know of is useful for every conceivable purpose. There is no model to help understand all models, just as there is no language that would enable you to understand all languages. The still-photo structural functionalist model, as well as the slow-motion film conflict model, are useful for understanding relationships and activities within social systems and between social groups. (They would help explain my question: What does the mother-child interaction of nurturing mean relative to the social group in general?) But a further question remains. What about the individual in the group? How and why do mothers come to know they are mothers and then act accordingly? How and why do fathers, children, bankers, physicians, hoboes, the sick, the well, the rich, the poor—how and why do all of these take on their social roles and play them out the way they do within social systems?

If you will recall, according to the structural functionalist model and its flip-side, the conflict model, a social system is a group of interacting persons whose interaction is structured and oriented around common concerns or purposes. This definition describes, at a high level of abstraction, what the previous models will get to see and describe, and how they will explain behavior. Now here is another definition of a social system. A social system is a system of symbols which acts to establish powerful, pervasive, and long-lasting moods and motivations in people, formulating conceptions of value-objects, and clothing these conceptions with such an aura of factuality that the moods and motivations are perceived to be uniquely realistic. In this definition the social system is a system of symbols, i.e., meanings, values, and feelings about these meanings and values that are attached to, embodied in and by persons, things, and events. The social system, as system of symbols, consists of persons (self and others), things (nature, time, space), and events (activities of persons and things) that have a symbolic reality. People do not simply respond to situations; rather they respond to the way they read and define the situation in terms of what they expect in and from the situation. The range of meaning within a situation (exiting from a supermarket) is interpreted symbolically by persons defining the situation. (The person exiting from a supermarket just shoplifted, just purchased groceries, just quit her job in the supermarket, just made out in the back room with the manager, etc.). However, no symbol can mean anything. (The person exiting from the supermarket cannot be said to be leaving his house, building a garage, operating on a cancer victim, etc., ad infinitum—it is always easier to be infallibly wrong then approximately correct.) The symbol gets its range of meaning from shared social expectations, from the shared social symbol system, much as words get their meaning from the shared social speech system. This sort of model that would analyze social systems in terms of the symbols that comprise them is called the *symbolic model* (to some extent, also called symbolic interactionist model).

The symbolic model presupposes that human individual and group behavior is organized around the symbolic meanings and expectations that are attached to objects that are socially valued. Such socially valued objects include the self, others, nature, time, space, and the All (God). Any existing person or group is a complex of symbolic patterns that at least temporarily maintains both personal and social equilibrium (like the structural functionalist model), but which requires continual readjustment in new and shifting situations (like the conflict model). These readjustments include slight to great alterations of ideas, values, moods, attitudes, roles, and social organization. Thus the symbolic model presupposes that for the most part, human interactions are symbolic interactions. People are always wrapped in social roles, sets of social rights and obligations relative to others. These symbolic roles situate people in relation to others, give them social status, e.g., the status of mother, father, son, daughter, rich, poor, and the like. The social system then turns out to be a patterned arrangement of role-sets, status-sets, and status-sequences consciously recognized and regularly at work in a given society. Social structures thus keep people apart, bring them together, define differences, point up similarities, and constrain and facilitate action.

From the standpoint of the symbolic model, a good way to understand our group of foreigners is to find out what roles, significant symbols, gestures, and definitions of situations our texts express or imply. What symbols embody the cultural cues of perception? What sorts of interaction take place between high-class and low-class people, and how do people define themselves in their various classes?

In what follows, what I plan to do is use models from various anthropologists who have studied Mediterranean society or societies similar to the ones we find in our texts. Some of these anthropologists use structural functionalist models, others use conflict models, and still others use symbolic models. I will pick and choose among them in order to try to understand various and broad areas of behavior. By laying out models in various areas of life, by showing how these models are implied or expressed in our texts, I would hope to lead you to add to the examples I present. Our common purpose is to understand this hypothetical group of foreigners represented by the New Testament texts. Our understanding will be in terms of the why's of their behavior, in terms of behavior typical of their culture. The adequacy of our understanding will depend upon the adequacy of our models. I would invite you to validate the model, to see if they do indeed explain, and to realize the spread of cultural difference that separates us from first-century Christians. The various areas I have chosen to consider might serve you as a set of glasses you can put on when you read the texts. You should find that you can see much better what was going on in that social world, how and why people behaved the way they did, what they considered significant and important in life. When you take those glasses off and return to our twentieth-century Western society, you will be faced with another social world, with a different set of hows and whys of human behavior, a different set of what people consider significant and important in life.

If the differences between their social world and ours prove too great, the variance between their moral judgments and ours too disturbing, the focus between their religious concerns and ours too distant, the chances are good that our interpretation has a higher probability of being more accurate. After all, our foreigners are foreigners, alien human beings, from a distant place and a distant time.

Summary

Trying to understand the writings of the New Testament in an adult, scholarly way is much like trying to understand a group of foreigners somehow dropped in our midst. Nearly all scholarly aids to understanding the Bible offer information about who, what, when, where, and how regarding these foreign writings. Such information is valuable and highly necessary. However, most of us need a why sort of answer to feel satisfied that we do in fact understand.

To answer a why question in relation to human social behavior, our own culture provides us with a truism as a starting point: All human beings are entirely the same, entirely different, and somewhat the same and somewhat different at the same time. The area of sameness asks why questions about the physical environment and about man as part of that physical environment: this is nature. The area of difference asks why questions about unique individuals and their unique personal stories: this is person. The area of partial similarity and partial difference asks why questions about the human environment people have developed as the framework or model of their social behavior: this is culture.

Cultures symbol people, things, and events in such a way that all persons in the group share the patterns of meaningfulness that derive from this symboling process. These patterns or cultural cues are assimilated and learned in the enculturation process, much as we all learn and assimilate the patterns of speech common to our group. For purposes of understanding, cultural stories might be broken down into the cultural cues that people assimilate. Such cues include those of perception, feeling, acting, believing, admiring, and striving.

The process of breaking down complex human activity for the purpose of understanding it, like breaking down a cultural story into its constituent cues, is called modeling. Models are generated because human beings, after puberty, can think abstractly. Models in human thought are simple, abstract representations of human experiences and interactions which are often highly complex. Models are made for purposes of understanding. Cultural anthropology has as its main focus to understand cultures other than our own by means of formulating adequate models, models that are neither superficial nor inaccurate. The so-called scientific method serves as a check on models. In cultural anthropology, three main types of models are used: the structural functionalist, the conflict or coercion type, and the symbolic.

In the remainder of the book, a number of specific models will be presented, mostly of the symbolic sort. After the models are presented, some examples will be given with the hope that you yourself will check out the adequacy of the model on the basis of information provided in the New Testament texts.

2

Honor and Shame:
Pivotal Values of the
First-Century Mediterranean World

To get a handle on what it means to study cultural patterns, you might try imagining the world as empty and void, without distinguishing features like rivers and mountains, rocks and trees—just one big smooth and even place. Think of it all like the trackless, vast land of a limitless desert. Now imagine a group of people coming on the scene. With their hands in the supple sand, they start making lines to indicate to each other that this side is "my side," that side is "your side." Another group comes along, makes a line, and declares that this side is "our side," that side is "your side." The wind comes and covers over the explicit lines, yet all continue to act as though they were still there, implicit in the sand. What happens in such line drawing? Etymologically, the words "define" and "delimit" refer to the process of drawing lines, setting up boundaries between inside and outside, hence between insiders and outsiders.

Meaning-building is like contriving lines in the shapeless stuff of the human environment, thus producing definition, socially shared meaning. Such lines obviously are drawn through and around time (hence the social times of childhood, adolescence, adulthood, retirement) and space (hence the social spaces often implicitly marked by the "boundaries" between the United States and Canada, your house and your neighbor's). What is not so obvious is that socially contrived lines are likewise drawn within and around people (the social lines that mark off self from others, that mark off roles and statuses), nature (the socially contrived lines that mark off all the stuff we study in the sciences, in economics, that we experience in our physical environment), and God or gods (the socially contrived lines marking off who or what we believe to hold it all together).

We are all born into systems of lines that mark off nearly all of our experiences. Such lines define the self, others, nature, time, space, and God/gods. It is probable that people bother to make such lines because we human beings have an overpowering drive to know where we are. Line-drawing enables us to define our various experiences so as to situate ourselves, others, and everything and everyone that we might come into contact with. Our ancestors passed down to us the set of lines they inherited, and with this we find ourselves in a cultural continuum that reaches back to the sources of our cultural heritage.

If you think about it, such line-drawing is rather arbitrary and can be highly ambiguous, charged with conflicting meaning. When I draw a line between me and you, what does that mean? Does it mean you can never come to my side without fear of conflict? Does it mean your side is of less value than my side? Does it mean we can never change the lines once they are drawn? Since the lines are socially contrived and since they can be highly ambiguous, such boundary markers are often a source of anxiety and conflict as well as of satisfaction and fulfillment. For example, think of the time-line marking age sixty-five. Does it mark satisfaction and fulfillment of a life of work, or rejection and uselessness? Does it lead to a period of reward or a period of punishment? The set of social lines we assimilate in the enculturation process provides all of us with a sort of socially shared map that helps and urges us to situate persons, things, and events with special emphasis on the boundaries. It shows us that there is a place for everyone and everything, and it teaches us that persons and things out of place are abnormal. For example, take good old country farm dirt. Dirt in the field is in its proper place, but when the same dirt gets into your house, the house is considered "dirty," unclean, impure, profaned. Dirt is matter out of place. Return it to where it belongs and your house is clean, pure, sacred once again. People out of place are called deviants. They too are considered unclean, impure, profaned. We often lock up deviants in a sort of social garbage can so as to keep our community clean, pure, sacred, unpolluted, and hence safe. In a later chapter we shall deal with clean and unclean, sacred and profane, at greater length. At this point I would like to consider three sets of person-lines that come together and are perceived to flow together quite consistently in the Mediterranean world. These three boundary markers are called power, sexual status, and religion, and where they come together, what they mark off, is something called *honor*.

Let me define power, sexual status, and religion. Power means the ability to exercise control over the behavior of others. Power is a symbol; don't confuse it with physical force. Don Corleone in *The Godfather* was a rather old and weak man with little physical force; yet he had much power and could control the behavior of others. Your parents and teachers often control your behavior without the use of physical force; they use power, a symbol standing for very real unpleasant and pleasant consequences for the persons under its sway. Sexual status (or roles) refers to the sets of duties and rights—what you ought to do and what others ought do to or for you—that derive from symboling biological, sexual differentiation. Are male "oughts" the same as female "oughts"? Is the way people ought to treat a male the same as they ought to treat a female? Sexual status refers to the male and female "oughts" recognized in a social group. Finally, by religion I mean the attitude and behavior one is expected to follow relative to those who control one's existence. This is what religion meant to people in the first-century Mediterranean world. Bible translations call it piety, and sometimes justice or righteousness. Who in fact had immediate control of your existence? Parents. Who had control of their existence? Grandparents. Who presently controls both you and your parents and grandparents? Various local, state, and national government officials; various employers, and the wealthy in the halls of power. And who controls all these, who is at the top of the ladder? The one who holds it all together, our God or gods. Now the proper attitudes of respect and homage, along with the behavior you are expected to follow in relation to those who controlled and control your existence, is what religion is about in the first-century New Testament world.

Understanding Honor

Honor might be described as socially proper attitudes and behavior in the area where the three lines of power, sexual status, and religion intersect. If this all sounds a bit too abstract (which it is—remember we are working on a model), then try this approach. Honor is the value of a person in his or her own eyes (that is, one's claim to worth) *plus* that person's value in the eyes of his or her social group. Honor is a claim to worth along with the social acknowledgment of worth. Society shares the sets of meanings and feelings bound up in the symbols of power, sexual status, and religion. Whom you can control is bound up with your male and female roles, which are also bound up with where you stand on the status ladder of your group. When you lay claim to a certain status as embodied by your power and in your sexual role, you are claiming honor. For example, a father in a family (sexual role, status on the ladder of society) commands his children to do something, and they obey (power): they treat him honorably. Other people seeing this would acknowledge that he is an honorable father. But should this father command and his children disobey, they would dishonor him, and his peers would ridicule him, thereby acknowledging his lack of honor as a father. Try another example. Say a teacher (in the first century all teachers are male = sexual status; the role of teacher likewise presupposes standing in the community of men, i.e., status on the social ladder) sets out a teaching which his disciples do not agree with; they do not acknowledge his teaching power. To bystanders, this would be an occasion of dishonoring him, since even his disciples do not believe him. Should his disciples believe him, see the truth of his teaching, accept what he says on his authority, then the bystanders of the community would acknowledge that he is in fact a teacher, hence worthy of honor. One more example. Say a young man elopes with the daughter of an honorable father. What would the daughter's behavior mean? The father as father (sexual role) has the right and duty to decide on the marriage of his daughter; she is embedded in his family, as it were. The daughter must acknowledge her father's status relative to her, since this is his religious rank on the status ladder. Be eloping, the daughter acts out the symbol of disregarding her father's power over her; she dismisses and disregards his authority, his power. What will the community say about the father's claim to social standing, his honor? Of course his daughter dishonored him, and the community would deny his claim to honor, since he could not even control his daughter as fathers should.

Honor, then, is a claim to worth *and* the social acknowledgment of that worth. For a person in such a society, there is a constant dialectic, a thinking back and forth between the norms of society and how the person is to reproduce those norms in specific behavior. A person constantly thinks about what he or she ought to do, about what is ideally acknowledged in the society as meaningful and valuable, and then examines his or her actions in the light of those societal norms and oughts. When a person perceives that his or her actions do in fact reproduce the ideals of society, he or she expects others in the group to acknowledge this fact, and what results is a grant of honor, a grant of reputation. To honor a person is to acknowledge publicly that his or her actions conform with social oughts. Honor as pivotal value in a society implies a chosen way of conduct undertaken with a view to and because of entitlement to certain social treatment in return. Other people not only say that a person is honorable; they also treat that person in the way that honorable persons are treated. It is something like our credit rating. A good credit rating makes money available, allows a person to incur debt and acquire goods for immediate use, and reflects upon a person's social standing in our society. What the first-century person was interested in was his or her honor rating. The right and title to worth is the right to status, and status (one's set of rights and obligations) derives from the recognition of one's social identity. Consequently, one who is in society depends upon his honor rating, which situates the person òn the status ladder of the community.

Thus a person's claim to honor requires a grant of reputation by others before it becomes honor in fact. If a person's claim to honor because of some action results in no social grant of reputation, then the person's action (and frequently the person him/herself) is labeled ridiculous, contemptuous, foolish, and is treated accordingly. (Note the use of the words "fool" and "foolish" in Proverbs, Ecclesiastes and the New Testament.) So the problem of honor for the person claiming it revolves about how, by whom, and on what grounds others will judge and evaluate his actions as worthy of repute.

How Does a Person Get a Grant of Honor?

Honor, like wealth, can be ascribed or acquired. *Ascribed honor*, like ascribed wealth, is honor that you get simply for being you, not because of anything you did for it. For example, if you should inherit a bundle, that would be ascribed wealth. Should you be born into a very wealthy family, that too would be ascribed wealth. Should someone you never met before give you a million, that would be ascribed wealth. Ascribed honor, then, is the socially recognized claim to worth that befalls a person, that happens passively, so to say. In this category, honor derives from the fact of birth ("Like mother, like daughter," Ezek. 16:44; "like father, like son," Matt. 11:27; see also Deut. 23:2; 2 Kings 9:22; Isa. 57:3; Hos. 1:2; Ecclesiasticus 23:25–26; 30:7). Being born into an honorable family makes one honorable, since the family is the repository of the honor of past illustrious ancestors and their accumulated acquired honor. One of the major purposes of genealogies in the Bible is to set out a person's honor lines and thus socially situate the person on the ladder of statuses. Genealogy points to one's ascribed honor (thus Matt. 1:2–16; Luke 3:23–38; questions about Jesus' family and origin look to the same thing in Mark 6:3; Matt. 13:54–57; Luke 4:22; John 7:40–42; for Paul read Rom. 11:1; Phil. 3:5).

Honor can also be ascribed to a person by notable persons of power. It can be ascribed by God, the king, aristocrats, in sum, by persons who can claim honor for others and can force acknowledgment of that honor because they have the power and rank to do so. Thus Jesus, as an utterly shamed and disgraced crucified person, is ascribed honor from God because God raised him, thus indicating His good pleasure in Jesus. John's Gospel articulates this view most clearly, since for John, Jesus' death is an exaltation, a glorification. The statement that Jesus "sits at the right hand of God" is the same assessment. For Paul, Christians can also expect such ascribed honor (Rom. 8:17–30).

Acquired honor, on the other hand, is the socially recognized claim to worth that a person acquires by excelling over others in the social interaction that we shall call challenge and response. Challenge and response is a sort of social pattern, a social game, if you will, in which persons hassle each other according to socially defined rules in order to gain the honor of another. Honor, like all other goods in first-century Mediterranean society, is a limited good (see chapter 4 below). There is only so much to go around, or at least that is what people learn to perceive. Now since honor is the pivotal value (much like money in our society), nearly every interaction with non-family members has undertones of a challenge to honor.

How Honor Is Acquired

Challenge and response is a sort of constant social tug of war, a game of social push and shove. You might look at it as a type of social communication, for any social interaction is a form of communication in which messages are transferred from a source to a receiver. Some person (source) sends a message by means of certain culturally recognized channels to the receiving individual, and this produces some sort of effect. The source here is the challenger, while the message is a symboled thing (a word, a gift, an invitation) or event (some action) or both. The channels are always public, and the publicity of the message guarantees that the receiving individual will react in some way, since even his non-action is publicly interpreted as a response. Consequently, challenge-response within the context of honor is a sort of interaction in at least three phases: (1) the challenge in terms of some action (word, deed, or both) on the part of the challenger; (2) the perception of the message by both the individual to whom it is directed and the public at large; and (3) the reaction of the receiving individual and the evaluation of the reaction on the part of the public (see Figure 2 and the explanation that follows).

The challenge is a claim to enter the social space of another. This claim may be positive or negative. A positive reason for entering the social space of another would be to gain some share in that space or to gain a cooperative, mutually beneficial foothold. A negative reason would be to dislodge another from his social space, either temporarily or permanently. Thus the source sending the message—always interpreted as a challenge—puts out some behavior, either positive (like a word of praise, a gift, a sincere request for help, a promise of help plus the actual help) or negative (a word of insult, a physical affront of various degrees, a threat along with the attempt to fulfil it). All such actions constitute the message that has to be perceived and interpreted by the receiving individual as well as the public at large.

The receiver looks upon the action from the viewpoint of its potential to dishonor his self-esteem, his self-worth. He has to judge whether and how the challenge falls within the socially acknowledged range of such actions, from a simple questioning of self-esteem to an outright attack on self-esteem to a total denial of self-esteem. Perception of the message is a sort of second step. It is very important to note that the interaction over honor, the challenge-response game, *can take place only between equals*. Hence the receiver must likewise judge whether he is equal to the challenger, whether the challenger honors him by regarding him as an equal as is implicit in the

Figure 2: *Challenge and Response*

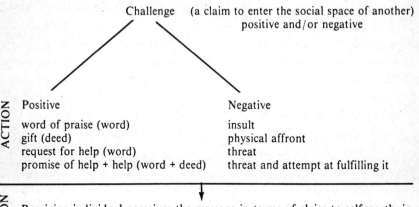

Challenge   (a claim to enter the social space of another)
positive and/or negative

ACTION

Positive	Negative
word of praise (word)	insult
gift (deed)	physical affront
request for help (word)	threat
promise of help + help (word + deed)	threat and attempt at fulfilling it

PERCEPTION

Receiving individual perceives the message in terms of claim to self-worth, in terms of potential dishonor to self-esteem in a range running from simple questioning of self-esteem to attack on or denial of self-esteem.

The individual must judge his perception in terms of usual publicly acknowledged criteria or norms of judging.

Receiving individual now must respond, assured that a public verdict will immediately follow with grant or rejection of honor.
The response or reaction runs a range as follows:

REACTION

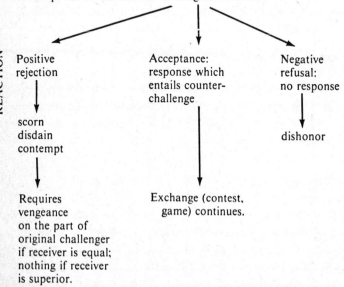

Positive
rejection

Acceptance:
response which
entails counter-
challenge

Negative
refusal:
no response

scorn
disdain
contempt

dishonor

Requires
vengeance
on the part of
original challenger
if receiver is equal;
nothing if receiver
is superior.

Exchange (contest,
game) continues.

challenge, or whether the challenger dishonors him by implying equality when there is none, either because the receiver is of a higher level or a lower level. Thus in the Gospels, the various learned groups that challenge Jesus imply that he is their equal. On the other hand, the high priest and Pilate do not regard Jesus' activity as a challenge, but rather as an annoyance by an inferior who can be swept aside.

The third step in the interaction would be the reaction to the message, involving the receiver's behavior that enables the public to pass a verdict: a grant of honor taken from the receiver of a challenge and awarded to the successful challenger, or a loss of honor by the challenger in favor of the successful recipient of the challenge. Any reaction on the part of the receiver of a challenge comprises his response. Such responses cover a range of reactions, from a positive refusal to react, through acceptance of the message, to a negative refusal to react. By this I mean that a person receiving the challenge message can refuse the challenge positively by a display of scorn, disdain, or contempt. If he is inferior or equal to the challenger, that would require the challenger to take steps to obliterate the insulting response, since such a response locates the challenger as an inferior. On the other hand, the receiver can accept the challenge message and offer a counter-challenge, and the exchange between them will continue. Or finally, the receiver can react by offering nothing by way of response; he can fail or neglect to respond, and this would imply dishonor.

The challenge, then, is a threat to usurp the reputation of another, to deprive another of his reputation. When the person challenged cannot or does not respond to the challenge posed by his equal, he loses his reputation in the eyes of the public. People will say he cannot or does not know how to defend his honor. He thus loses his honor to the challenger, who correspondingly gains in honor. This set of cultural cues of perception, action, and belief is symboled in the behavior of conquering kings who take on the titles of the ones they vanquish. It is likewise symboled in the behavior of the early Christians, who applied to the resurrected Jesus all the titles of those who were to overcome evil and death: Messiah, Lord, son of David, Son of God, and the like.

Now in the first-century Mediterranean world, every social interaction that takes place outside one's family or outside one's circle of friends is perceived as a challenge to honor, a mutual attempt to acquire honor from one's social equal. Thus gift-giving, invitations to dinner, debates over issues of law, buying and selling, arranging marriages, arranging what we might call cooperative ventures for farming, business, fishing, mutual help, and the like—all these sorts of interaction take place according to the patterns of honor called challenge-response. Because of this constant and steady cue in Mediterranean culture, anthropologists call it an *agonistic* culture. The word "agon" is Greek for an athletic contest or a contest between equals of any sort. What this means, then, is that the society we are considering is a society that looks upon all social interactions outside the family or substitute family (circle of friends) as a contest for honor. Since honor and reputation, like all goods in life, are limited, then every social interaction of this type comes to be perceived as an affair of honor, a contest or game of honor, in which players are faced with wins, ties, and losses.

Honor Symboled by Blood

Honor is always presumed to exist within one's own family of blood, i.e., among all those one has as blood relatives. A person can always trust his blood relatives. Outside that circle, all people are presumed to be dishonorable, guilty, if you will, unless proved otherwise. It is with all these others that one must play the game, engage in the contest, put one's own honor and one's family honor on the line. Thus no one outside the family of blood can be trusted until and unless that trust can be validated and verified. So men of the same village or town who are not blood relatives relate to each other with an implied deep distrust which in practice prevents any effective form of cooperation. Strangers to the village, that is, people of the same cultural group but not resident in the same place, are looked upon as potential enemies, while foreigners, that is, those of other cultural groups just passing through, are considered certain enemies. Consequently, any interaction or conversation between two unrelated men or two unrelated women (the sexes usually don't mix) are engagements in which both sides probe for the least hint of the other's intentions or activities. Such interactions are not concerned with sociability, but rather are expressions of opposition and distance.

Honor Symboled by Name

Such sentiments of opposition, distance, and exclusiveness among fellow villagers and their families find a more extended expression in competition for name and honor. Again, name and honor hold the central concern of people in every context of public action and give purpose and meaning to their lives, like money does in our society. From another point of view, good name and family honor are also central, because families in the first-century world were not entirely self-sufficient and independent economically. Social life requires some degree of interdependence, cooperation, and shared enterprise. In Mediterranean society, such extra-familial cooperation takes the form of a free association of a contractual kind. In biblical terms, people made implicit or explicit covenants with each other. Now with whom would you enter into any sort of cooperative covenant or contract? For example you can't buy anything on hire purchase unless your credit rating is good enough. In the Mediterranean world no one would freely associate with you in covenant relationship unless your honor rating were good, so that good name and prestige are the most valuable of assets (see ch. 4 below).

By and large, then, competition for prestige and honor takes the form of an ongoing contest, an ongoing rivalry, an ongoing win, tie, or lose game in which *both* how you play and whether you win or not are equally important. Attempts to damage reputations are constantly made, yet great stress is laid on face-to-face courtesy in terms of formalities. The prestige level of the members of the community is a matter of continual comment. Every quarrel normally leads to imputations of acts and intentions that are dishonorable—and that have nothing to do with the quarrel. Prestige derives from the domination of persons rather than things. Hence any concern people show for the acquisition of goods derives from the purpose of gaining honor through generously disposing of what one has acquired among equals or socially useful lower-class clients. In other words, honor is acquired through beneficence, not through the fact of possession and/or the keeping of what one has acquired. Thus money, goods, and any sort of wealth are really a means to honor, and any other use of wealth is considered foolish.

Consequently, the honorable person is one who knows how to and can maintain his or her social boundaries in the intersection of power, sexual status, and respect for others, including God. The shameless person is one who does not observe social boundaries. The fool is one who takes a shameless person seriously. Specifically, then, how is honor displayed and recognized?

How Honor Is Displayed and Recognized

You will recall that the set of social boundaries that we assimilate through enculturation provides us with a sort of socially shared map that enables and urges us to situate persons, things, and events within proper boundaries. Now this social road map is most often condensed and expressed in somewhat compact symbolic form in one's physical person. What I mean—and I shall return to this point later—is that your physical person, your body, gets symboled as a sort of personalized road map of the social values of our society. For example, as our social road map marks off my house from your house, giving free access to your house to those who are and can be intimate with you, similarly, the ones who have free access to touching, kissing, and caressing you (your physical person) will generally be those who have free access to your house. Your physical person replicates your general social space, your house. By replication I mean the use of similar and often identical patterns of behavior in different domains. Back to our example, just as you can let service personnel into your house for specific purposes, so you can let service personnel have limited access to your physical person for specific purposes: the plumber or electrician for the house; the physician or dentist for your physical person. The rules for interaction with service personnel are generally very similar. In each case you must allow intimacies in areas that are normally private, in each case the personnel are duly licensed, in each case the personnel are paid for their services in money to signify that the transaction is over, complete, with no lingering debt of interpersonal obligation—even if you feel grateful to the person who stopped the flooding in your basement or helped you walk again. This sort of replication, the presence of identical rules in different domains, is rather common in cultures. To return to the discussion of honor, the physical person (the body) is normally a symboled replication of the social value of honor. The head and front of the head (face) play prominent roles. To be seated at the head of the table, to be at the head of the line, to head an organization, are so many replications of crowning the head, of others taking off their hat to you, of others bowing their head in your presence. Honor and dishonor are displayed when the head is crowned, anointed, touched, covered, uncovered, made bare by shaving, cut off, struck, or slapped. The symbolic nature of the face, a part for the whole, is much like that of the head, with the added dimension of the spatial *front*, the focus of awareness. To *affront* someone is to challenge him in such a way that the person is and cannot avoid being, aware of it; the challenged person in an affront is obliged to witness the challenge to his face. In return, the recognition of the challenge takes place on the face. In Semitic culture, this focus of recognition is the center of the face, the nose: the Hebrew word for anger refers to flared nostrils, and a reference to flared nostrils is most often translated "wrath."

To put it mildly, a physical affront is a challenge to one's honor; unanswered it becomes a dishonor in the judgment of persons witnessing the affront. Physical affronts symbol the breaking of required social and personal boundaries, thus causing resentment. Resentment means the psychological state of feeling distressed and anxious because the expectations and demands of the ego are not acknowledged by the actual treatment a person receives at the hands of others. It is a sense of moral indignation at the perceived injustice in the behavior of others toward me—not in keeping with my power, sexual status, and social role. In brief, they refuse to recognize my honor and prestige, and their physical affrontery symbols that refusal. They have crossed into the social space that is me.

To bring things back to normal, what is required is a response, a sort of pushing another to his own side of the line, along with a fence-mending operation. This process of restoring the situation after the deprivation of honor is usually called satisfaction or getting satisfaction. To allow one's honor to be impugned, hence taken, is to leave one's honor in a state of *desecration*—out of place, unclean, impure—and this would leave a person socially dishonored and dishonorable. On the other hand, to attempt to restore one's honor, even if the attempt is unsuccessful, is to return it to the state of the sacred, to purify or cleanse it, leaving one socially honored and honorable (hence a man of valor, of standing).

Again, it is very important to note that according to the social patterns of the honor contest, not everyone can engage in the game. According to the rules or code, *only equals can play*. Only an equal can actually challenge another in such a way that all perceive the interaction as a challenge. Only an equal—who must be recognized as such—can impugn a person's honor or affront another. The reason for this is that the rules of the honor contest require that challengers stand on equal social terms. Thus an inferior on the ladder of social standing, power, and sexual status does not have enough honor to resent the affront of a superior. On the other side, a superior's honor is simply not committed, not engaged, by an inferior's affront, although the superior has the power to punish impudence. Thus a man can physically affront his children or wife, a high-class person can strike a low-class person, free men can buffet slaves, the occupying Roman army can make sport of most low-class citizens. These interactions do not imply an honor contest in themselves. (They may imply the honor of another, e.g., the patron who is to protect the interests of his clients, but this complicates things at this point; we will refer to it later.) In other words, in the social game of honor, a man is answerable for his honor only to his social equals, to those with whom he can, in the perceptions of the society, compete.

To get back to physical affronts, any physical boundary-crossing on the part of another presumes and implies the intention to dishonor. In honor societies, actions are more important than words, and how one speaks is more important than what one says. In physical affrontery, the challenge to honor is presumed to exist unless it is clearly and totally apparent that no challenge is intended (e.g., a child striking an adult). Yet to claim that one did not intend dishonor (e.g., by saying "I didn't mean it" or "excuse me") is to require a certain indulgence on the part of the one affronted, and this indulgence may or may not be granted. Much would depend upon the degree of dishonor involved (how, in what circumstance, where did a person strike or touch another), the status of the person challenging (who did the striking), and the degree of publicity (what audience witnessed the event).

Again, publicity, witnesses, are crucial for the acquisition and bestowal of honor. Representatives of public opinion must be present, since honor is all about the tribunal or court of public opinion and the reputation that court bestows. Literally, public praise can give life and public ridicule can kill.

Honor and the Interpretation of a Challenge

It should be obvious by now that two levels of interpretation are involved in the challenge and ripost of honor: (1) that of the individual challenged—his or her estimation of the intention and status of the challenger; (2) that of the public witnessing the challenge—their interpretation of the intention and status of the challenger and the challenge in the public forum. Given these two necessary elements, there will be various styles of challenging, running from a direct affront through indirect challenges of rather ambiguous challenges.

To deal with the last first, the style called an *ambiguous affront* is a challenging word or deed put forth "accidentally on purpose." For example, I may "accidentally" bump into you and knock you down, or I may say that someone else said that your daughter is a fine whore. This sort of challenge puts the one challenged in a dilemma. He must decide what the community will judge the challenge to be, for the victim of an affront or challenge is dishonored only when and where he is forced by the public to recognize that he has been challenged and did not respond. This is where swearing or non-legal oath-making comes into play. The purpose of such swearing (e.g., in business: "I swear to God this is a healthy jackass") is to eliminate ambiguity and make explicit one's true intentions. An oath activates a type of implicit curse (e.g., if the jackass is sick and dies, God will punish me for calling Him to witness to an untruth, hence for dishonoring Him). And public opinion judges a person dishonored if he or she does not submit to an oath. (Read the law regarding a wife suspected of adultery in Num. 5:11–31; see also Luke 1:73; Acts 2:30; 23:12, 14–21; Heb. 7:20–28; the antithesis in Matt. 5:33–37 looks to oath-making in business.) If one makes an oath to another, then only the oath maker, not the other person, can be dishonored after the oath; but the oath, like the word of honor, must be freely made to engage the game of challenge and response.

What then is a word of honor? A person can commit his honor in the contest of life only by sincere intention. To demonstrate this sincerity of intention, this steadfastness of purpose, he can give his word of honor, which functions like an oath or swearing, but only engages the individual him/herself, not God or others. Such a word of honor is only necessary for outsiders who find what a person says or does ambiguous or incredible. Jesus' characteristic "truly, I say to you" seems to function like a word of honor (cf. Matt. 5:18,26; 6:2,5,16; 8:10; 10:15,23,42; 11:11; 13:17; 16:28; 17:20; 18:3,13,18,19; 19:23,28; 21:21,31; 23:36; 24:2,34,47; 25:12,40,45; 26:13,21,34; Mark 3:28; 8:12; 9:1,41; 10:15,29; 11:23; 12:43; 13:30; 14:9,18,25,30; Luke 4:24; 12:37; 18:17,29; 21:32; 23:43; John 1:51; 3:3,5,11;

5:19,24,25; 6:26,32,47,53; 8:34,51,58; 10:1,7; 12:24; 13:16,20,21,38; 14:12; 16:20,23; 21:18).

The reason for giving a word of honor is that moral commitment in telling the truth unambiguously in such honor cultures derives from the social commitment or loyalty to persons to whom such commitment is due. In first-century limited-good society, there was no such thing as universal, social commitment (e.g., the brotherhood of all men). Rather, the right to the truth and the right to withhold the truth belong to the man of honor and to contest these rights is to place his honor in jeopardy, to challenge him. Lying and deception are or can be honorable and legitimate. To lie in order to deceive an outsider, one who has no right to the truth, is honorable. On the other hand, to be called a liar by anyone is a great public dishonor. The reason for this is that truth belongs only to one who has a right to it. To lie is to deny the truth to one who has a right to it, and the right to the truth only exists where respect is due (in the family, to superiors, and not necessarily to equals with whom I compete or to inferiors). Thus to deceive by making something ambiguous or to lie to a person is to deprive the other of respect, to refuse to show him honor, to humiliate him. And one may lie to a person one is prepared to challenge, to affront. It is not dishonoring for a person to affront another man, equal or inferior.

The boundary lines marking off a person in some way likewise include all that the person holds worthwhile and worthy. What this means is that along with personal honor, an individual shares in a sort of collective or corporate honor. Included within the bounds of personal honor are all those worthies who control a person's existence, i.e., patrons, king, and God—all whom one holds vertically sacred. Also included is one's family—the horizontally sacred. The reason for this is that like individuals, social groups possess a collective honor.

And just as honor is personal or individual as well as collective or corporate (e.g., family honor, national honor, and the like), so another way to challenge a person is by means of what might be called a corporate affront. Instead of affronting you, I affront someone intertwined with your honor. Reaction to a challenge and the consequent deprivation of honor of someone other than the person in question can only happen when that person's honor is involved in some way. This can happen by dishonoring another's wife (who is perceived as embedded in her husband), dishonoring his extended family (like his father or blood cousin in his presence), or even dishonoring those socially judged to be unable to defend their honor personally. The Bible often refers to these socially defenseless persons— orphans, widows, and, before Deuteronomy, resident aliens—as people incapable of defending their own honor. The aged and infirm who are males are marginal cases. Then there are those who are socially barred from responding to challenges to their honor because of their unequal, superior, exalted status, e.g., one's highly placed patron, the king, or God (gods). Thus a person may take up the challenge to his king or God because they are intertwined in his own honor.

As mentioned earlier, a dishonored person must attempt to restore his honor. It is the attempt that counts, not the actual restoration of the status previously held. We might call this attempt "satisfaction," and satisfaction is not the same as triumph. In the movie *Rocky,* the hero gets a sort of satisfaction in the end, although he loses the fight in a bloody way. What is required and suffices for satisfaction in our honor society is (1) that the one dishonored has the opportunity to achieve satisfaction, and (2) that he follows the rules of the game in doing so. Satisfaction then has the nature of an ordeal, implying a judgment of destiny or fate of God's sanction. If the dishonored person or his family does not follow the socially approved rules, then the challenge-response game is over, and feud or war results.

Honor and Going to Court

Furthermore, it is considered highly dishonorable and against the rules of honor to go to court and seek legal justice from one's equal. This too reduces the challenge-response code to a feud or war. First of all, the one challenged and taking his action to court only aggravates his dishonor (what the challenger did to him) by publicizing it. Further, satisfaction in court, legal satisfaction, does not restore one's honor because (1) to go to court is to demonstrate inequality, vulnerability, and puts one's own honor in jeopardy; (2) court procedure allows those who deprived you of honor to gloat over your predicament; and (3) to have the court obtain recompense or ask for an apology from another is dishonoring in itself, implying that one cannot deal with one's equals. Honor demands restoration or satisfaction by oneself or extended self. To appreciate this, note how in our society—or in movies depicting segments of our society—those above or outside the law, like the very wealthy, street gangs, organized criminals, the Mafia, are a sort of law to themselves and avoid being dishonored in their interactions by recourse to normal legal procedures. In the first-century world, normal legal procedures are used to dishonor someone or some group perceived to be of higher, more powerful status, and recourse to them is an admission of inequality. This inequality, of course, can be highly ambiguous, and again, it is up to public opinion to dole out the honor.

Dimensions of Collective Honor

Since first-century societies did not consider individualism a pivotal value as we do (cf. chapter 3), collective or corporate honor was one of their major focuses. Social groups, like the family, village, or region, possess a collective honor in which the members participate (note John 1:46: "Can anything good come out of Nazareth?"; Titus 1:12: "Cretans are always liars, evil beasts, lazy gluttons."). This perception might be expressed as "I am who I am and with whom I associate." Depending upon the dimensions of the group, which can run a replicating range from individual, nuclear family, to kingdom or region, the *head* of the group is responsible for the honor of the group with reference to outsiders, and symbolizes the group's honor as well. Hence members of the group owe loyalty, respect, and obedience of a kind which commits their individual honor without limit and without compromise. There are two types of groupings, natural and voluntary.

Natural groupings depend upon circumstances over which the individual has no control, e.g., birth, residence, nationality, social class. In natural groupings, a person's intentions to belong to the group are of no importance at all. One is born physically and symbolically into the group, and there is nothing one can do about it. The grouping is not the result of any free choice, competition, or contract. What this means is that one belongs naturally, by blood, so to say, to the group, and this very fact obliges the person to respect, observe, and maintain the boundary lines, the definitions, the order within the group.

In order to understand the assessments of honor within natural groupings, recall what I said previously about the varying range of the challenge message. Challenges are not all of the same degree or quality, but move along a spectrum from a simple invitation to share a cup of wine to an extreme like murder. Just as there are varying degrees of challenge, so too the response reaction ought to be at least of the same quality as the challenge for the person involved to maintain his honor.

I would like to distinguish, for clarity's sake, three hypothetical degrees. These degrees of challenge would depend upon whether the challenge to honor is revocable or not, whether the boundaries can be readily repaired or not, whether the implied or actual deprivation of honor is slight, significant, or extreme and total. Thus challenges or transgressions of the boundaries marking off the person run within three degrees. The first degree involves extreme and total dishonor of another with no revocation possible. This is outrage and would include murder, adultery, kidnapping, total social degradation of a person by depriving him of all he needs for his status, in sum, all the things listed in the second half of the Ten Commandments, for this in fact is what is listed there: outrages against one's fellow Israelite that are simply not revocable but require vengeance. The second degree would be a significant deprivation of honor with revocation possible, e.g., by restoring stolen items, by making monetary restitution for seducing one's unbetrothed, unmarried daughter, and the like. The third and lowest degree of challenge to honor would be the regular and ordinary interactions that require normal social responses, e.g., repaying a gift with one of equal or better value, allowing another to marry my children if he lets my children marry his. In other words, any implicit or explicit dishonor must allow for satisfaction commensurate with the degree of dishonor present.

Now to return to our natural groupings, note that any sort of first-degree dishonor done within the group is considered sacrilegious and comprises a category of transgression quite out of the ordinary. Those controlling our existence in natural groupings are sacred, religious persons. Thus, murdering a parent is not simply homicide, it is parricide, parent-killing. the same with murdering a king (regicide) and, in the Middle Ages, murdering a pope (papacide). Such crimes against members of one's natural groupings, against those who share in one's honor, are always felt to be extremely grievous and socially disorienting. On the other hand, homicide committed on outsiders is not sacrilegious and might even be meritorious, as in defense of the group's honor in war—and often in peace. Outsiders are not sacred. The Romans called the crime of first-degree transgression in natural groupings *nefas,* and branded the perpetrator *sacer* (literally, "sacred"), meaning the gods would certainly get him for what he did. Like natural groupings of family, village, region, and class are aristocracies and the feudal relations between wealthy landowners and resident tenants, patrons and clients.

Voluntary groupings, on the other hand, depend upon a person's choices and result from contracts, quasi-contracts, or competition. In voluntary groupings, the persons involved have no sacred qualities as persons because of who they are in relationship to others. Rather, the posts or offices in such groupings bear the qualities otherwise embodied by persons in natural groupings. While internal opinion as well as public opinion are at work in natural groupings, in voluntary groupings public opinion is sovereign. Some such voluntary groupings in the first century would be trade guilds, municipalities (systems of villages), city-states with republican forms of government, voluntary burial organizations, Palestinian parties like Pharisees, Sadducees, Essenes, Zealots, and the like. Perhaps the early groups of Christians likewise looked upon their groups as voluntary associations like the Palestinian parties after whom they often modeled themselves.

From the viewpoint of collective honor, depending on the quality of the grouping, the sacred persons or posts have power over all the dimensions of honor in their respective groups. They arbitrate questions of value; they delimit what can be done or maintained without sacrilege; they define the unconditional allegiance of the members. This is what Jesus and Paul did for the voluntary groupings that formed around them; this is what the rabbis did for the voluntary groupings that adhered to them; and this is what the emperor in Rome or the high priest in Jerusalem did for the natural groupings under their power. Thus these sacred persons or sacred post-holders themselves symbol both social honor—they have precedence relative to others in their groups—and ethical honor—they are perceived to be implicitly good and noble. The reason for this is that social honor or precedence (being head of something/someone) is normally readily convertible into ethical honor or implicit goodness, just as capital or collateral assures credit in our money system. Honor (social precedence) guarantees against dishonor (immoral or ignoble ethical bearing). Thus the king of the nation (or the father of the family) simply cannot be dishonored within the group; he is above criticism. What he is guarantees the evaluation of his actions. Any offense against him only stains the offender.

Further, the king in his kingdom (like the father in his family) can do no wrong because he is the arbiter of right and wrong. Any criticism apart from conventional, usual ones is rated an act of disloyalty, a lack of commitment. No one has a right to question what the king decides to do, just as no individual in the group has any right to follow what he or she might personally think is right or wrong. The king (father) must be followed and obeyed; he is sufficient conscience for all concerned. This proper attitude is symboled in rituals of honor, and one must pay honor (worship originally meant worthiness, a recognition of worth) even if one does not feel inclined to. On the other hand, honor felt is honor paid, and honor paid indicates what ought be felt. In sum, honor causes a society to derive what ought be done from what in fact is done. That is, the social order as it should be is derived from the social order as it actually is. Paying honor to those to whom it is owed legitimates established power and further integrates societal members in their system of obligatory consent.

Honor and the Moral Division of Labor: The Double Standard

As mentioned previously, honor refers to the intersection of the societal boundaries of power, respect for those in statuses above us, and sexual roles. What I have said to this point, for the most part, looks to power, respect, and the male sex. What is the role of the female in the game of honor? By and large, the honor of the natural group is divided up into what may be called a sexual or moral division of labor. This sexual division of labor looks mainly to the family and kinship group but can be replicated in other dimensions of life.

To understand this point, let us begin with the heavy sexual symbol of such societies. First of all, male honor is symboled by the testicles, which stand for manliness, courage, authority over family, willingness to defend one's reputation, and refusal to submit to humiliation. (How does this relate to the eunuch parable in Matt. 19:12; See Lev. 21:20; Deut. 23:1; 25:11; Jer. 5:8; Ezek. 23:20; cf. also Amos 5:2–6.) Female honor, on the other hand, is symboled by the maidenhead (hymen) and stands for female sexual exclusiveness, discretion, shyness, restraint, and timidity. The male clearly lacks both the physiological basis for sexual exclusiveness or sexual "purity" (he cannot symbolize invasion into his space as the female can), and his masculinity is in doubt if he maintains sexual purity, i.e., if he does not challenge the boundaries of another through their women. Females, for their part, symbol their purity by thwarting off even the remotest advances to their symbolic space, yet it is the responsible male's duty to protect, defend, and look after the purity of his women (wife, sister, daughter), since their dishonor directly implies his own.

The division of honor into male and female corresponds to the division of roles in the family of husband, wife, and children. This aspect of family is called the family of procreation, to distinguish it from the family from which the individuals came—called the family of orientation. In the family of procreation, honor delegates implicit goodness or virtue as expressed in sexual exclusiveness to females, and social precedence with the duty of defending female sexual exclusiveness to the males. This sort of division of honor gets replicated in arrangements of space. (Remember: replication means the same patterns or rules in different areas.)

Female space or female things—the places where females are allowed, the things that females deal with exclusively, like kitchen utensils, drawing water, spinning and sewing, bread baking, sweeping out the house, etc.—all these female spaces and things are centripetal to the family dwelling or village of residence. That means they face toward the inside, with a sort of invisible magnet of social pressure turning females inward, toward their space in the house or the village. All things taken from the inside to the outside are male; all things remaining on the inside are female. The places of contact between the inside and outside (the family courtyard, the village square, or the area by the city gate) are male when males are present, although females may sometimes enter either properly chaperoned or when males are present. In this arrangement, the wife normally becomes financial administrator with the key to the family chest when and since the husband must go out—to fields, to other villages, on pilgrimage. However, males who must go out for protracted periods of time without their females, like traders, traveling merchants, certain types of shepherds, wandering preachers, and the like, necessarily leave their honor in doubt, since their wives are left alone for rather long periods.

Consequently, the honor of the male is involved in the sexual purity of his mother (although his father has the main obligation in this regard), wife, daughters, and sisters—but not in his own sexual purity. According to this pattern, then, *the sexual purity or exclusiveness of the female is embedded within the honor of some male.* The male is responsible for the maintenance of this sexual exclusiveness; it is delegated to the male, so to say. Hence the woman remains with her own responsibility alleviated, unless she courts disaster by stepping out of socially acceptable boundaries. Thus the honorable woman, born with the proper sentiment of shame which she inherits from her mother ("Like mother, like daughter." Ezek. 16:44), strives to avoid the human contacts which might expose her to dishonor. She cannot be expected to succeed in this endeavor unsupported by male authority and control. This perception underlies public opinion, which makes the deceived husband or father the object of ridicule and dishonor, and entitles them to avenge any outrage committed against them in this way. Furthermore, women not under the tutelage of a male—notably widows and divorced women—are viewed as stripped of female honor, hence more like males than females, therefore sexually predatory, aggressive, "hot to trot," hence dangerous. Only remarriage would restore their true sexual roles, but often this is not socially possible. Hence the precarious position of the widow and divorcee (and the importance of a bill of divorce enabling and entitling the woman to a new marriage if this can be arranged for her). This cultural attitude toward widows is clearly articulated in 1 Tim. 5:3–16.

Toward Defining Honor and Shame

As mentioned previously, honor means a person's (or group's) feeling of self-worth and the public, social acknowledgment of that worth. Honor in this sense applies to both sexes. It is the basis of one's reputation, of one's social standing, regardless of sex. In this common context, where honor is both male and female, the word "shame" is a positive symbol, meaning sensitivity for one's own reputation, sensitivity to the opinion of others. To have shame in this sense is an eminently positive value. Any human being worthy of the title "human," any human group worthy of belonging to the family of man, needs to have shame, to be sensitive to its honor rating, to be perceptive to the opinion of others. A sense of shame makes the contest of living possible, dignified, and human, since it implies acceptance of and respect for the rules of human interaction. On the other hand, a shameless person is one who does not recognize the rules of human interaction, who does not recognize social boundaries. The shameless person is one with a dishonorable reputation beyond all social doubt, one outside the boundaries of acceptable moral life, hence one who must be denied the normal social courtesies. To show courtesy to a shameless person makes one a fool, since it is foolish to show respect for boundaries when a person acknowledges no boundaries, just as it would be foolish to continue to speak English to a person who does not know the language at all.

One can speak of honor and shame of both males and females only as they pertain to those areas of social life covering common humanity, specifically, natural groupings in which males and females share a common collective honor: the family, village, city, and its collective reputation. However, actual, everyday, concrete conduct that establishes one's reputation and redounds upon one's group is never independent of the sexual or moral division of labor. Actual conduct, daily concrete behavior, always depends upon one's sexual status. At this level of perception, when

Figure 3: *Honor and Shame: Moral Division of Labor*

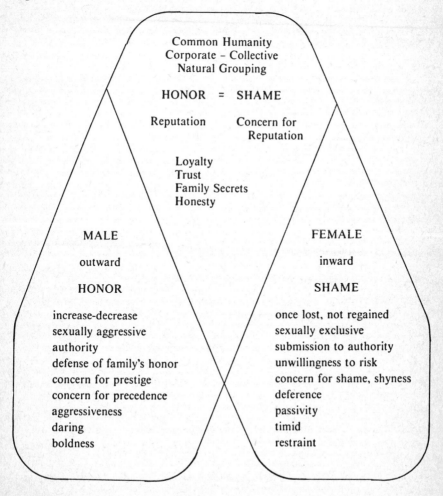

Common Humanity
Corporate – Collective
Natural Grouping

HONOR = SHAME

Reputation   Concern for
                Reputation

Loyalty
Trust
Family Secrets
Honesty

MALE   FEMALE

outward   inward

HONOR   SHAME

increase-decrease   once lost, not regained
sexually aggressive   sexually exclusive
authority   submission to authority
defense of family's honor unwillingness to risk
concern for prestige   concern for shame, shyness
concern for precedence   deference
aggressiveness   passivity
daring   timid
boldness   restraint

honor is viewed as an exclusive prerogative of one of the sexes, then honor is always male, and shame is always female. Thus in the area of individual, concrete behavior (and apart from considerations of the group), honor and shame are sex-specific. This is a sort of lower level of abstraction at which individual males symbol honor and individual females symbol shame (see Figure 3).

At this level of abstraction, male honor is symboled in the testicles and covers typically male behavior, running from the ethically neutral to the ethically valued: manliness, courage (the willingness to challenge and affront another male), authority, defense of the family's honor, concern for prestige, and social precedence—all this is honorable behavior for the male. Female shame, on the other hand, is symboled in the maidenhead and likewise covers a range running from the ethically neutral to the ethically valued: feelings of sensitivity or "shame" to reveal nakedness, shyness, blushing, timidity, restraint, sexual exclusiveness—all this is positive shame for the female and makes her honorable.

To move up once again to a higher level of assessment in which honor and shame refer to both males and females, people acquire honor by personally aspiring to a certain status and having that status socially validated. On the other hand, people *get shamed* (not *have* shame) when they aspire to a certain status and this status is denied them by public opinion. At the point a person realizes he is being denied the status, he is or gets shamed, he is humiliated, stripped of honor for aspiring to an honor not socially his. Honor assessments thus move from the inside (a person's claim) to the outside (public validation). Shame assessments move from the outside (public denial) to the inside (a person's recognition of the denial). To be or get shamed, thus, is to be thwarted or obstructed in one's personal aspiration to worth or status, along with one's recognition of loss of status involved in this attempt.

Again, as a common value, applicable to natural groupings, honor runs a range from internal goodness to social precedence or power. The wicked, powerful king has honor in terms of social precedence, while the good but poor and powerless family has honor in terms of ethical goodness. Assessments of honor along this sort of spectrum take a replicating twist that might help us understand enduring shame—the weeping and gnashing of teeth in Matthew, for example. For any fusion of male and female elements in a higher level symbol can always unravel into its constituent parts. What I mean is that just as a female who loses her shame gets shamed and therefore no longer has shame but is shameless, so also natural groups can lose their shame by getting shamed to such an extent that they no longer have shame but are shameless. Certain families and institutions (e.g., husbands serving as pimps, first-century tavern and inn owners, actors, prostitutes as a class) are considered irretrievably shameless. The reason for this is that they respect no lines of exclusiveness and hence symbol the chaotic. In this sense, when honor is viewed as a common value, emphasis on its aspects as internal goodness (the female aspect) may lead to a judgment according to which once it is lost, it can never be regained—exactly like female sexual exclusiveness. On the other hand, emphasis on its aspects as social precedence or power (the male aspect) may lead to a judgment according to which honor can be increased or decreased at the expense of others. Such fluctuating honor will be used as a gauge of social standing.

With the family as repository of natural honor, marriage, as we shall see, is always the fusion of the honor of two families. Honor as shame or ethical goodness comes from the mother; she symbols it. Honor as social precedence comes from the father; he symbols it. The fusion of honor in an honorable marriage thus makes up the social inheritance with which the new family of procreation gets set to play the game of life.

Summary

From a symbolic point of view, honor stands for a person's rightful place in society, his social standing. This honor place is marked off by boundaries consisting of power, sexual status, and position on the social ladder. From a structural functionalist point of view, honor is the value of a person in his or her own eyes plus the value of that person in the eyes of his or her social group. Honor is a claim to worth along with the social acknowledgment of worth. The purpose of honor is to serve as a sort of social rating which entitles a person to interact in specific ways with his or her equals, superiors, and subordinates, according to the prescribed cultural cues of the society.

Honor can be ascribed or acquired. Ascribed honor befalls or happens to a person passively through birth, family connections, or endowment by notable persons of power. Acquired honor is honor actively sought and garnered most often at the expense of one's equals in the social contest of challenge and response. Figure 2 describes this type of interaction, which is a sort of conflict model.

Honor, both ascribed and acquired, is often symboled by blood (one's blood relations, group) and name. A good name fundamentally means adequate honor to carry on the social interactions necessary for decent human existence. Honor is frequently symboled by certain physical features and the treatment given one's physical person. Physical affronts are always symbolic affronts that require a response. Failure to respond means dishonor, disgrace. Just as the head and features of the head symbol a person's honor, so also does the head of a group symbol the honor of that group. For honor has both individual and corporate or collective dimensions. Whenever the honor of another is bound up with an individual's own honor, that individual is required to defend and represent the honor of all bound up with him. This sort of collective honor is to be found in natural and voluntary groupings. Natural groupings, like ascribed honor, befall a person and depend upon circumstances beyond the person's control. Relations within the natural grouping are sacred, blood, or pure relationships that tie persons directly together. Voluntary groupings, like acquired honor, result from calculated choices. Relationships within voluntary groupings are focused on posts and functions, and these posts and functions are considered sacred and pure, although many different people can hold them. The heads of both natural and voluntary groupings set the tone and embody the honor rating of the group, so to say.

Honor has a male and a female component. When considered from this perspective, the male aspect is called honor, while the female aspect is called shame. Shame in this context refers to a person's sensitivity about what others think, say, and do with regard to his or her honor. In natural groupings, honor and shame—the male and the female—are fused, like in the family, village, or city. Such natural groupings have collective honor and shame. But in the moral division of labor, in the concrete activity of concrete people, honor and shame become sexually specific, sexually embedded. The male is to defend both corporate honor and any female honor embedded in the corporate honor. The female, on the other hand, symbols the shame aspect of corporate honor, that positive sensitivity to the good repute of individuals and groups. Figure 3 illustrates this point.

Testing the Hypothesis

Like all models, the picture of honor and shame, along with the challenge-response interaction typical of that picture, has to be tested out. If the model covers all instances of honor and shame behavior in the New Testament, then it will have been validated and prove to be an adequate model. It is now up to you to test out the model, disprove it if you like. But if it works, then what sort of meaning behind the behavior in the texts would you say it yields?

To test out the model, you might begin by looking up the vocabulary of honor and shame in a concordance to the New Testament. I am using the Revised Standard Version for what follows. And a perusal of an R.S.V. concordance offers the following:

1) honor: equivalents include glory, blamelessness, repute, fame (and verbs like to honor, glorify, spread the fame, etc.)
2) shame: disgrace, dishonor (and the verbs to shame, be ashamed, feel ashamed)

3) dishonor: scorn, despise, revile, reproach, rebuke, insult, blaspheme, deride, mock (and actions like striking the head, spitting upon, etc.)
4) intention to challenge: test, entrap, entangle (and questions indirectly addressed to Jesus by being addressed to his disciples; questions that are obviously mocking, normally those of the Sadducees in the Gospels)
5) perceptions of being challenged or shamed: vengeance, wrath, anger, the vocabulary of sin (transgression, offense, sin, wrong) with a person as object.

The concordance enables you to find where such words are used; now you would have to look up the entire passage to see what sort of behavior is described, then check this behavior against the model. Does the model help you flesh out what is only implicit in the passage?

Perhaps an easier way to test out the model is to stick to one New Testament writing. For example, take the Gospel of Mark with the purpose of picking out and explaining the honor and shame interactions explicit and implicit in the text:

—As you read the whole of Mark, note how Jesus' fame spreads, how public approval of him mounts from the outset of his ministry up to the passion, e.g., Mark 1:28; 6:33; 6:54.

—Why do people come up to Jesus and kneel (Mark 1:40; 10:17; 15:19) or worship (= kneel) him (Mark 5:6)?

—In the episode of Herod, Herodias, and the daughter, what sort of honor-shame interaction goes on? What is the meaning of his oaths? Is the daughter like her mother (Mark 6:14–29)?

—Why does the interaction of Jesus and the Syrophoenician woman take the turn that it does in the dialogue (Mark 7:25 ff.)?

—Note the arguments on who is greater (more honorable) in Mark 9:33 ff. and 10:36 ff. Why this concern among the disciples?

—Consider some of Jesus' debates with his opponents. What do they indicate about Jesus' honor (e.g., Mark 2—3:15; 7:1–13; 11:27–33; 12:13–17; 12:18–27; 12:38–40)?

—Take the parable in Mark 12:1–9: how does it follow honor-shame rules, with increasing outrage and predictable outcome?

—In terms of honor-shame interactions, what is the meaning of the fact that Jesus' enemies take him to trial? How does the trial prove Jesus to be honorable? What is the meaning of Mark 14:65; 15:17–20? What do Peter's denial and oath mean in terms of honor-shame in Mark 14:66–72?

Does the model make sense of all the data?

Again, in terms of honor and shame, what does "fool" or "foolish" mean in the following: Matt. 7:26; 23:17; 25:2,3,8; Luke 11:40; 24:25; Gal. 3:1,3; and in Paul's sarcasm in 2 Cor. 11:16,17,19,21; 12:6,11. What of Eph. 5:17; Titus 3:3; James 2:20; 1 Peter 2:15? Is being a fool the same as being naive, ignorant, unknowledgeable, as in our culture? Or is a fool one who wilfully lacks respect for social boundaries, a moral failure?

You might also consider Paul's Letter to the Galatians and First Corinthians. Does Paul consider himself ahead of these churches in terms of natural groupings or voluntary groupings (read Gal. 4:19; 1 Cor. 4:15)? Is his attitude about his standing in the group shared by others? Is he offended because some in the group listen to other apostles? Why would this be a challenge to him? What is the honor-shame meaning of the piece of autobiography in Gal. 2:1–14? Of 1 Cor. 11:2–16; 1 Cor. 11:18–22? What is the meaning of the "wrath of God" in Rom. 1:18 ff.? How does Rom. 1—3 indicate that God has been outraged?

3

The First-Century Personality:
The Individual and the Group

Honor and shame are pivotal values in the social world of the New Testament and of the Bible as a whole. In that social world, the virtuous man is the strong man who knows how to maintain and perhaps increase his honor rating along with that of his group. If we move from our consideration of these pivotal values to the individuals who embodied them, we would be moving from a discussion of a phase of social interaction to a sort of social psychology, to the self-image and mind-set of the honorable or dishonorable man.

The First-Century Personality

What sort of personality sees life nearly exclusively in terms of honor? For starters, such a person would always see himself or herself through the eyes of others. After all, honor requires a grant of reputation by others. So what others tend to see is all-important. Further, such an individual needs others for any sort of meaningful existence, since the image he has of himself has to be indistinguishable from the image of himself held and presented to him by his significant others in the family, village, city, or nation. In this sense, a meaningful human existence depends upon the individual's full awareness of what others think and feel about him, along with his living up to that awareness. Literally, this is conscience. The Latin word *conscientia* and the Greek word *syneidesis* stand for "with-knowledge," that is, a knowledge with others, individualized common knowledge, commonly shared meaning, common sense. Conscience then refers to a person's sensitive awareness to his public ego-image with the purpose of striving to align his own personal behavior and self-assessment with that publicly perceived ego-image. A person with conscience is a respectable, reputable, and honorable person. Respectability, in this social context, would be the characteristic of a person who needs other people in order to grasp his or her own identity. Conscience is a sort of internalization of what others say, do, and think about one, since

51

these others play the role of witness and judge. Their verdicts supply the person with grants of honor necessary for a meaingful, humane existence.

Thus the honorable man would never expose his distinct individuality, his unique personhood, his inner self with its difficulties, weaknesses, confusions, and inabilities to cope. Rather, he knows how to keep his psychological core hidden and secret. He is a person of careful calculation and discretion, normally disavowing any dependence on others. He is adept at keeping his innermost self concealed with a veil of conventionality and formality, ever alert to anything that might lead to his making an exhibition of himself, to anything that would not tally with the socially expected and defined forms of behavior that have entitled him to respect. Typically, for example, Paul tells the Corinthians that he rejects the opinions that men might form of him (1 Cor. 4:1–4), yet he seeks the approval of his significant others, the Corinthians in this case, for what he does (1 Cor. 9:1 ff.). Jesus, too, is depicted as a man of honor, "not regarding the face [= honor] of men" (Mark 12:14), yet concerned about "who . . . men say that I am" (Mark 8:27; see also Matt. 11:2–6, 7–14; 16:13–16).

Given this brief description of the first-century personality, what sort of individual would you expect to find in the pages of the New Testament? Would this person be like us and feel guilty when he did something wrong? Could he be said to have the kind of conscience we do? Our sort of conscience, as most folks use the word, refers to the pain we feel within ourselves over some past specific action that we ourselves, individually and alone, judge to be "bad" because it was "wrong." Would our first-century person be worried about past specific actions he himself judged to be wrong? Or would he be worried about actions that he thought other people might say would be dishonoring? These sorts of questions are rather important, since they lead us to forming some sort of assessment of the group of foreigners who people our New Testament texts.

Consider the Apostle Paul, for example. For many Christians today, Paul is a perfect example of a person much like we conceive ourselves to be, affected by anxiety and guilt, by remorse and concern for atonement and spiritual development. For he must have been introspective, meditative, and habituated to examining his conscience before God. Did he not write: "So I find it to be a law that when I want to do right, evil lies close at hand. For I delight in the law of God, in my inmost self, but I see in my members another law at war with the law of my mind and making me captive to the law of sin which dwells in my members" (Rom. 7:21–23)? But is he pointing to some sort of internalized standard of morality, some sense of personal guilt, to a self-punitive, self-critical reaction of remorse and anxiety after the transgression of some commandment of God? Certainly St. Augustine (d. 430) and, much later, Martin Luther, thought so. However, the general problem with their interpretation is that Paul believed that the Law was observable and that he himself did not transgress the commandments of God in the Law. As a matter of fact, in a brief autobiographical passage in Phil. 3, Paul himself tell us that "as to righteousness under the law," he considered himself "blameless" (v. 6; read the whole passage). In other words, he believed that during his pre-Christian period of life, he actually observed all that was required of him by the Law. Hence it was not guilt or anxiety relative to the Law that led him to Christianity or maintained his Christian conversion. But how did he know he was blameless? Was it because his conscience did not bother him? Or was it because none of his significant others, none of his publics, accused him of acting shamefully, dishonestly, or disobediently? What sort of self-awareness does Paul reveal in his writings? What sort of self-awareness was typical of first-century Mediterranean man?

In order to generate some understanding of first-century personality, I have chosen two models from cultural anthropology that seem to fit the data in our texts. The first of these models deals with the non-individualistic, dyadic self-awareness that seems to have been typical of the first-century people in our New Testament. The second sketches out the conception of the makeup of the individual that seems to have been characteristic of the Semitic subculture of that period and earlier. Taken together, the models should offer some understanding of the dynamics running between the individual and the group as we find them in the New Testament.

Dyadic Personality

Have you ever noticed how very few people bother to read any first-century Mediterranean writings apart from the New Testament? For the most part, people who do in fact read and study the New Testament do so because they believe that it is the Word of God, and that therefore it should be read. Yet if the New Testament lacked the theological, religious imprint that it bears, how many persons in our culture would find it enticing, alluring, and interesting reading? Would they be turned on by reading Plutarch, Josephus, Philo of Alexandria, Epictetus, Musonius Rufus and other writers of that period? By our standards, first-century Mediterranean writings are generally boring. Perhaps the main reason for this is that the center of concern in those writings is not ours. For whenever we start to discuss some gossip, some person, or some social problem, almost invariably and inevitably our conversation takes on psychological undertones. We adopt a point of view that is psychological. Why do some of your friends take drugs? Why are some people in your school homosexual? Why that senseless suicide? Why is your aunt's or uncle's marriage on the verge of a breakdown? Why don't you ever have fun? Why did your friend get invited on a date, but not you? Why do certain persons always get better grades, better jobs, make more friends? Why do certain people always keep their grades and salaries secret? How many of these kinds of questions will you answer without resorting to psychology, to questions of inner motivations that are quite personal, to reasons based on personality, personality development, interpersonal ability in terms of poise, IQ, emotional control, personal story, highly personal reasons, and the like?

In our culture, we tend to consider a person's psychological makeup, his or her personality development from infancy on, as well as his or her individuality and uniqueness (personal reasons), as perhaps the most important elements in understanding and explaining human behavior, both our own and others'. Yet if you carefully read the New Testament writings or any other writing from the same period and place, you will find an almost total absence of such information. One obvious reason for this state of affairs is that the people described in the New Testament, as well as those who described them, were not interested in or concerned about psychological or personality information. Otherwise we should find as much of such information in those writings as we might in a modern biography, novel, or newspaper. Since this kind of information is lacking, you might conclude that the first-century Mediterranean person did not share or comprehend our idea of an "individual" at all. And I believe you would be right.

What do we, in fact, mean by an "individual"? Clifford Geertz has observed that our conception of the individual as " . . . a bounded, unique, more or less integrated motivational and cognitive universe, a dynamic center of awareness, emotion, judgment and action organized into a distinctive whole and set contrastively both against other such wholes and against its social and natural background, is, however incorrigible it may seem to us, a rather peculiar idea within the context of the world's cultures." You might not have thought this is what you think you are like, but take the time to consider this description of an individual. In our culture we are brought up to stand on our own two feet, as distinctive wholes, distinctive individuals, male and female. We are motivated to behave in the "right" way, alone, if necessary, regardless of what others might think or say. In our process of identity formation, we tend to believe and act as though we do so singly and alone, responsible only for our own actions, since each person is a unique sphere of feeling and knowing, of judging and acting. When we relate to other people, we feel that they are as distinct and unique beings as we ourselves are. In addition to being unique and distinct persons, each of us lives within our unique social and natural environments. This is individualism, and this sort of individualism is rare in the world's cultures today. It was perhaps totally absent from the New Testament.

Instead of individualism, what we find in the first-century Mediterranean world is what might be called "dyadism" (from the Greek word meaning a pair, a twosome). A dyadic personality is one who simply needs another continually in order to know who he or she really is. The person I described at the beginning of this chapter (you might read it again) is a dyadic personality. Such a person internalizes and makes his own what others say, do, and think about him because he believes it is necessary, for being human, to live out the expectations of others. That person would conceive of himself as always interrelated to other persons while occupying a distinct social position both horizontally (with others sharing the same status, moving from center to periphery) and vertically (with others above and below in social rank). Such persons need to test this interrelatedness, with the focus of attention away from ego, on the demands and expectations of others who can grant or withhold reputation. Pivotal values for such persons would be honor and shame, not guilt.

The dyadic personality is an individual who perceives himself and forms his self-image in terms of what others perceive and feed back to him. He feels a need of others for his very psychological existence, since the image he has of himself must agree with the image formulated and presented by significant others, by members of significant and person-sustaining groups like family, village, even city and nation. To paraphrase Geertz, our first-century person would perceive himself as a distinctive whole *set in relation* to other such wholes and *set within* a given social and natural background. Every individual is perceived as embedded in some other, in a sequence of embeddedness, so to say. If our sort of individualism leads us to perceive ourselves as unique because we are set apart from other unique and set-apart beings, then the first-century person would perceive himself as unique because he was set within other like beings within unique and distinctive groups. If this all sounds a bit abstruse, consider the following situation. When you or almost anyone you might know enter a crowded room, say at a reception or party, more often than not you will feel and imagine that your immediate task is to solve the problem of group presence, the problem of community. How can you move from your inner self out across the no-man's land of group presence and make contact with another separate and unique person? This sort of problem is typical of individualism. For the first-century person, the problem is the opposite. How can one permanently embedded, psychologically and socially, in a group of significant others differentiate himself or herself to act as an individual at all? The dyadic personality is thus a person whose total self-awareness emphatically depends upon such group embeddedness.

For the dyadic personality, interpersonal behavior remains purely impersonal without some sort of perception that he or she and another person are somehow attached to each other, somehow related to each other. In other words, a basic prerequisite for a truly interpersonal exchange is that

I, as a dyadic personality, and another human being mutually believe that we have some common personal bonds, from shared blood to mutual acquaintances to common nationality and heritage. We have to come to see that somehow we are "brothers" or "kinsmen." Should there be nothing in common between us except our common humanity—even the sort of common humanity expressed in the Stoic brotherhood of males under the fatherhood of Zeus who indwells the individual male—then our interaction would remain impersonal, like an interaction with a tree or a tennis ball or a goldfish.

To get a better feel for the type of personality I am describing, imagine your name to consist of only your family name and your family's place of origin. Say your name, then, would be Smith of Chicago. (Note: This is only a device to get you to feel dyadic personality. In the first century no one bore a family name with place of origin as their name however, most people in the first-century Mediterranean world were in fact geographically immobile.) As Smith of Chicago, you would, of course, be only one particular instance of Smith of Chicago; there would be others. Yet the name "Smith of Chicago" would directly refer to what all you Smiths and Chicago have in common, to what is typical of your unique group. Hence, should I get to meet and know you, Smith of Chicago, I would really get to know a representative of a class, an abstract class known as Smith of Chicago. And this class would consist of enduring, lasting, and fixed qualities; all Smiths of Chicago from time immemorial would presumably have the same qualities you have. I would, naturally, presume that what I see in you is typical of all Smiths of Chicago, so if I got to know those qualities from you or any other Smith of Chicago, I would get to know all of you—by getting to know one of you. It is the group that is unique, individualistic, not the representative of the group.

Further, because both of us would refer to ourselves and perceive each other in terms of such specific group or class qualities, we would tend to believe and presume that human character as specified in unique and distinct groups and their individual components is fixed and unchanging. Every family, village, city, and nation would be quite predictable, and so would the individuals who are embedded in and share the qualities of some family, village, city, or nation. Consequently, if anything in life is unpredictable, it is not the individual. Rather, unpredictability derives from something or someone beyond the control of the predictable and unchanging human beings we might know. So there is no need to look inside the individual human being, either oneself or any other. In other words, it would make no cultural sense at all to ascribe anything to personal and uniquely individual psychological motives or introspectively generated reasons and motivations.

Another way to say this is that the dyadic personality makes sense out of other people by means of "sociological" thinking, by means of reasons typical of the group to which the individual belongs and whose values the individual embodies. By our standards, such "sociological" thinking would be based on extremely poor sampling techniques. We would call such perceptions "stereotypes," that is, fixed or standard general mental pictures which various groups mutually hold in common and which represent their expectations, attitudes, and judgments of other groups.

For example, consider the following statements: "Cretans are always liars, evil beasts, lazy gluttons" (Titus 1:12). "Jews have no dealings with Samaritans" (John 4:9). "O Jerusalem, Jerusalem, killing the prophets and stoning those who are sent to you" (Matt. 23:37; Luke 13:34). "Certainly you are one of them; for you are a Galilean" (Mark 14:70). "Can anything good come out of Nazareth?" (John 1:46). "Woe to you, Chorazin! woe to you, Bethsaida! . . . and you, Capernaum, will you be exalted to heaven?" (Matt. 11:21–24; Luke 10:13–15). "Is not this the carpenter, the son of Mary and brother of James and Joses and Judas and Simon, and are not his sisters here with us?" (Mark 6:3). Note how such statements derive their understanding of some person on the basis of family, village, or city in which individuals are embedded. The same sort of approach can be found in Paul when he talks of nations, of "Jews and Greeks" (e.g., Rom. 3:2–29; 9:24; 11:14; 1 Cor. 1:22–24; 9:20; 10:32; Gal. 2:13–15); in John's Gospel when the author speaks of the "Jews"; and in Revelation as the author stereotypes the Christian populace of the cities of Asia Minor to which the seven letters are addressed (Rev. 2—3). Thus to get to know one member of the group is to get to know the whole group. While many in our society do in fact make judgments of this sort, a culture that does not go beyond general "sociological" criteria would lack individualism in our sense of the word. And, it seems, the first-century Mediterranean world reveals such a culture.

Consider the characteristic ways of explaining behavior in our documents. Whenever anything significant happens, be it an occasion of joy or a human problem or crisis, the dyadic personality inevitably ascribes it to standard, "sociological," stereotypical causes (e.g., by citing a maxim or proverb: "*For* where your treasure is, there will your heart be also" [Matt. 6:21]) or to rather obvious, external, precipitating events (like Mark's "the girl got up and walked; *for* she was twelve years old" [5:42]; or the notice that Jesus found Peter and Andrew "casting a net into the sea; *for* they were fishermen" [Matt. 4:18]). At the close of this chapter, I will ask you to verify this point by considering a large sampling of "for" or "because" statements in the New Testament. None of these statements, to my knowledge, contains psychological, introspective, uniquely personal sorts of explanation, explanations that would be typically personal in our culture. It would seem that the New Testament (like the Bible in general) simply lacks any uniquely personal, individualistic motives or introspectively generated explanations for human behavior. Such explanations would be quite beside the point for the dyadic personality. Rather, the individual was symptomatic and representative of some group.

From this viewpoint, responsibility for morality and deviance is not an individual alone, but on the social body, the group in which the individual is embedded. It is because something is amiss in the functioning of the social body that individual deviance crops up. Thus, for example, Paul stigmatizes whole groups, Jews and Greeks (Rom. 1—3) or Galatians (Gal. 3:1) and sees some socially infecting *hamartia* (later called original sin) behind individual sinful actions. Mourning, the public protestation of the presence of evil, is a group reaction to deviance in its midst, as in 1 Cor. 5:1 ff.; 2 Cor. 12:21; Rev. 18:7–15.

Undoubtedly the moral norms we find in the New Testament have relevance for individual conduct, but in all such moral descriptions and listings, the individual is not the main concern. Such descriptions are written from the viewpoint of the supra-individual, objective horizon of the social body. Examples of such descriptions are the various sin lists (e.g., Mark 7:21–22 and parallels); lists of vices and virtues (e.g., Gal. 5:16–24); and household codes (e.g., Eph. 5:21—6:9; Col. 3:81—4:1; 1 Tim. 2:8—3:15). The main problem is to keep the family, the village, and the nation sound, corporately and socially. In Christian communities, the main problem was to keep the Christian group, the individual church, in harmony and unity, in sound state (e.g., 1 Cor. 12; Rom 12:3–21). The individual as such, our dyadic personality, is expendable (e.g., "It is expedient for you that one man should die for the people, and that the whole nation should not perish" [John 11:50]; Christian excommunication procedures in 1 Cor. 5:5, 13; Rom. 16:17; and Paul's own willingness to be cut off for his people, Rom. 9:3). Further, the soundness of the group, like the behavior of the dyadic personality individually, is heavily determined by its impact on surrounding groups and by the expectations of outsiders, for example, 1 Thess. 4:12; 1 Cor. 6:6; 10:32–33; 14:23; Rom. 12:17–18; Col. 4:5; 1 Tim. 3:7. Christians have to be at least as good as the outsiders are, and in this sense outsiders set the norm for the group.

Given this emphasis on dyadic personality and its concomitant honor and shame values, one of the chief implications we can deduce from these facts is that first-century people did not know each other very well in the way we know people, i.e., psychologically, individually, intimately, and personally. Again, this is due to the fact that they knew or cared little about psychological development, psychological motivations, and introspective analyses. Jesus himself, as presented in the texts of the Gospels, is a good example in this regard. Of the twelve men he chose, we are told that one betrayed him, one denied him, and the rest quibbled a lot and eventually abandoned him in a crisis situation. Paul himself constantly has problems with the allegiance of the various groups he gathered, e.g., the Galatians and the Corinthians. All this simply indicates what poor judges of individual character, of individual psychology, people in such cultures are. This is not because they are obtuse or unobservant. Rather, it is because such abilities are culturally unimportant; there are no cultural cues of perception highlighting this feature.

Conditions under which it would be advantageous to know people well as individuals are left out of cultural focus, so to say. For if one had to know other individuals very well, it would mean that people were idiosyncratic, inconstant, moody, devious, changeable, and unpredictable. It would mean, in sum, that people were not sensitive to their honor, to their conscience, to the image other people held of them and their group. So for the people of the New Testament period, if human beings are anything, it is certain that they are not "psychologically unique worlds," at least not to other human beings. For only God knows the human heart (Luke 16:15; Acts 1:24); can see what is secret (Matt. 6:4, 6, 18); can disclose what is in the heart (1 Cor. 14:25); tests our hearts (1 Thess. 2:4); searches the hearts of men (Rom. 8:27); and hardens the heart of whomever he wills (Rom. 9:18). That Jesus is said to have discerned what people had in their hearts is very significant in this regard (e.g., Luke 5:22; 9:47). However, it was culturally assumed that only God knew the individual heart, and yet this is not an expression of despair. It simply means that people do not have to know what is in another's heart because the uniquely personal is culturally defined as not very interesting, and it would have nothing to do with human relations anyway. It is what comes out of the heart that counts, the fruits that reveal the inmost quality of the tree (e.g., Mark 7:21–22; Matt. 7:16–20, and see below). Yet what in fact emerges from the heart is, as we might expect, stereotypical and culturally predictable.

If you were a student of psychology and were to evaluate the people presented in the New Testament, you would probably say that they were rigid and highly controlled personality types, or that they were fearful of others, or that they interacted in standardized and conventional ways almost all the time. You would categorize them as anti-introspective, or not at all psychologically minded. The whole point is that in this aspect of their culture, they were not like we are at all. So to infer psychological states of some person or other on the basis of our texts (e.g., the psychology of Jesus or Paul) would be a highly questionable and obviously anachronistic enterprise. There simply is not enough information in the text for this sort of inference.

In sum, the primary emphasis in the culture we are considering is on dyadic personality, on the individual as embedded in the group, on behavior as determined by significant others. Groups are unique and distinct. On the other hand, individual behavior was certainly evaluated, even if from a stereotypical point of view. Such evaluation presupposes some set of categories for perceiving and assessing behavior. Now what set of categories does the New Testament employ to function as a non-introspective model of the individual human being?

The Makeup of Man: A Three-Zone Model

Dyadic personality seems to have been common throughout the various cultures of the first-century Mediterranean world. At a rather high level of abstraction, these cultures were quite similar. Yet at a lower level of abstraction, at the level of the subcultures in the area, there were notable differences. Among these differences is the manner of articulating personality perception, i.e., the way in which people described the workings of the individual human being. Greek and Roman philosophers and their followers talked of the makeup of man in terms of body and soul, in terms of intellect, will, and conscience, in terms of virtues and vices that fazed a person's immortal soul. Such ideas and terminology are absent from the biblical writings. How then did the largely Semitic biblical authors perceive the stereotyped, non-introspective makeup of the dyadic personalities they described and interpreted in their writings?

As I mentioned previously, descriptions of human behavior in the New Testament depict persons and events concretely, from the outside, so to say. They avoid introspection as uninteresting, and evaluate behavior on the basis of externally perceptible activity and in terms of the social functions of such activity. Now what is the individual framework of typically human behavior, the makeup of the individual in himself or herself? Again, man is perceived as a socially embedded and interacting whole, a living being reacting to persons and things on the outside of the individual. The main framework of perimeters or boundaries of this interaction between the individual and the world outside the individual is described metaphorically, for the most part, using parts of the human organic whole as metaphors. Thus, most obviously, man is endowed with a heart for thinking, along with eyes that fill the heart with data; a mouth for speaking, along with ears that collect the speech of others; and hands and feet for acting. More abstractly, man consists of three mutually interpenetrating yet distinguishable zones of interacting with his environments: the zone of emotion-fused thought, the zone of self-expressive speech, and the zone of purposeful action.

To put it in other words, the way the human being is perceived as fitting into his rightful place in his environments, physical and social, and acting in a way that is typically human, is by means of his inmost reactions (eyes-heart) as expressed in language (mouth-ears) and/or outwardly realized in activity (hands-feet). These three zones comprise the non-introspective makeup of man and are used to describe human behavior throughout the Bible, from Genesis to Revelation. They are typical, in the first century, of the Semitic subculture of the Mediterranean world and perhaps underlay the philosophical accretions of the Greek and Roman worlds as well. Be that as it may, our concern here is with the biblical writings, and it is to them that we turn to verify this three-zone model. This model was invented and discovered by Bernard de Geradon over twenty years ago, and in what follows, many of his observations will be presented.

To begin with, it might be useful to recall that Semitic descriptive approaches tend to be highly synthetic rather than analytic—more like floodlights than spotlights. A floodlight covers a whole area at one time, and movement of the light might intensify exposure in a given part of the area, yet the whole area always remains in view. Similarly, specific words covering one of the three zones would stand for the whole zone, while always keeping the total functioning human being in view. Here is a representative list of such words and the zones they refer to:

1) *Zone of emotion-fused thought:* eyes, heart, eyelid, pupil, and the activities of these organs: to see, know, understand, think, remember, choose, feel, consider, look at. The following representative nouns and adjectives pertain to this zone as well: thought, intelligence, mind, wisdom, folly, intention, plan, will, affection, love, hate, sight, regard, blindness, look; intelligent, loving, wise, foolish, hateful, joyous, sad, and the like.

In our culture, this zone would cover the areas we refer to as intellect, will, judgment, conscience, personality thrust, core personality, affection, and so forth.

2) *Zone of self-expressive speech:* mouth, ears, tongue, lips, throat, teeth, jaws, and the activities of these organs: to speak, hear, say, call, cry, question, sing, recount, tell, instruct, praise, listen to, blame, curse, swear, disobey, turn a deaf ear to. The following nouns and adjectives pertain to this zone as well: speech, voice, call, cry, clamor, song, sound, hearing; eloquent, dumb, talkative, silent, attentive, distracted, and the like.

In our culture, this zone would cover the area we refer to as self-revelation through speech, communication with others, man the listener who dialogues with others in a form of mutual self-unveiling, and so on.

3) *Zone of purposeful action:* hands, feet, arms, fingers, legs, and the activities of these organs: to do, act, accomplish, execute, intervene, touch, come, go, march, walk, stand, sit, along with specific activities such as to steal, kidnap, commit adultery, build, and the like. The following

representative nouns and adjectives pertain to this zone: action, gesture, work, activity, behavior, step, walking, way, course, and any specific activity; active, capable, quick, slow, and so forth.

In our culture, this zone would cover the area of outward human behavior, all external activity, human actions upon the world of persons and things.

It seems almost impossible for us to tell whether persons using this model were explicitly aware of it. It seems more likely that the model served as an implicit pattern, an inarticulated set of significant areas working much like the grammar of a native speaker who knows no explicit, articulated grammar. Yet whenever a writer (or speaker in the text) describes human activity, he inevitably has recourse to the three zones, at times emphasizing only two of them or even one of them, with the others always in view in the background.

The idea is that all human activities, states, and behaviors can be and are in fact chunked in terms of these three zones. Now when all three zones are explicitly mentioned, then the speaker or writer is alluding to a total and complete human experience. For example, it is to such a total and complete experience that John alludes when he writes: "That which was from the beginning, which we have *heard,* which we have *seen* with our *eyes,* which we have *looked upon* and *touched* with our *hands,* concerning the word of life . . . that which we have *seen* and *heard* we *proclaim* also to you, so that you *may have fellowship*" (1 John 1:1–3). Similarly, the law of limited retribution in Exod. 21:24, restated in Deut. 19:21, and cited in part in Matt. 5:38, basically refers to limiting retribution within the whole range of human interactions: "*Eye* for *eye, tooth* for *tooth, hand* for *hand, foot* for *foot.*" The statement looks to righting restrictions put upon individual social rights. If this legal formula derives from and expresses the three zones that make up a human being, it would obviously not be meant literally and concretely (except by persons who do not understand the culture or by persons in the culture who are at the concrete stage of cognitive development, i.e., children and adults who are retarded by nature or by choice or experience).

A few more examples: "There are six things which the LORD hates, seven which are an abomination to him: haughty *eyes,* a lying *tongue,* and *hands* that shed innocent blood, a *heart* that devises wicked plans, *feet* that make haste to run to evil, a false witness who *breathes out lies,* and a man who sows discord among brothers" (Prov. 6:16–19). In this seven-patterned proverb (patterned much like the seven days of creation in Gen. 1), we have two complete descriptions of the totally wicked man in terms of three zones, followed by the worst type of person in that culture, one who breaks up bonds of loyalty in a family of blood. Or again, note how the prophet Elisha symbols his total living self as he lies upon the child he seeks to resuscitate:

"his *mouth* upon his mouth, his *eyes* upon his eyes, and his *hands* upon his hands" (2 Kings 4:34). Or consider the description of the linen-clothed man in Daniel, what is meant to be a total description: "His face like the appearance of lightning, his *eyes* like flaming torches, his *arms* and *legs* like the gleam of burnished bronze, and the sound of his *words* like the noise of a multitude" (Dan. 10:6). This is a statement of the total and complete function of the person described. The author of Revelation takes his cue from Daniel and describes his experience of the Son of man as follows: "His *eyes* were like a flame of fire, his *feet* were like burnished bronze, refined as in a furnace, and his *voice* was like the sound of many waters; in his right *hand* he held seven stars, from his *mouth* issued a sharp two-edged sword, and his *face* was like the sun shining in full strength" (Rev. 1:14–16). Again, we have a description of function in terms of three zones, a portrayal of how this being relates to those he comes into contact with—a functional picture. Note also how the final section of the Sermon on the Mount (Matt. 6:19—7:27), dealing with the righteousness of disciples, covers the three zones: the first block of material deals with the eyes-heart (Matt. 6:19—7:6), the second with mouth-ears (Matt. 7:7–11), and the last, exhorting section with hands-feet (Matt. 7:13–27).

As previously mentioned, at times only two of the zones are mentioned, leaving the third in the background. Thus, for example: "You have heard that it was said, 'You shall not *commit adultery* [hands-feet].' But I say to you that every one who *looks* at a woman lustfully has already committed adultery with her in his *heart* [eyes-heart]. If your right *eye* causes you to sin, pluck it out and throw it away; it is better that you lose one of your members than that your whole body be thrown into hell [eyes-heart]. And if your right *hand* causes you to sin, cut it off and throw it away; it is better that you lose one of your members than that your whole body go into hell [hands-feet]" (Matt. 5:27–30). Notice the chiastic pattern in this passage (a pattern in the form of the Greek letter X, thus: a, b, b', a'). Just as one cannot commit adultery with one's physical and literal hands and feet or with one's physical and literal heart, so too the right eye that needs to be plucked out and the right hand that needs to be cut off are not physical and literal eyes and hands. Rather, the parable urges that one consider the zones or spheres of activity that prove to be an obstacle to proper interpersonal behavior and "cut out" such activities. In this passage, only two of the zones are mentioned, thus emphasizing the relationship between the heart and the hands and feet, between one's interior, innermost self and one's outward activity. Mark 7:14–23 is much like this passage from Matthew. The basic argument about uncleanness and the heart is about the relationship between one's interior, innermost self and outward activity: activity flows from the heart, and it is the heart that needs realigning. The same holds for speech: "For out of the abundance of the *heart* the *mouth* speaks" (Matt. 12:34, and see Matt. 13:13–17).

The Makeup of Man and God

A tradition in the Jewish writing, *Pirqê Aboth* 2:1, exhorts: "Know what is above you: an all-seeing *eye*, an all-hearing *ear* and a book in which all your *actions* are recorded." The eye, ear, and recording of actions obviously pertain to God. Since statements about God, like statements in physical science, derive from analogies based on human behavior, it follows that biblical descriptions of how God functions will take the shape of analogies drawn from perceptions of how man functions.

Consider idols. Idols, of course, have *"mouths,* but they speak not, they have *eyes,* but they see not, they have *ears,* but they hear not" (Ps. 135:16–17); they "cannot either *see* or *hear* or *walk"* (Rev. 9:20). Now what about God? "He who planted the *ear,* does he not *hear?* He who formed the *eye,* does he not *see?* He who chastens the nations, does he not *chastise?"* (Ps. 94:9–10). Throughout the Bible, we read repeatedly about how God "is wise in *heart,* and mighty in *strength"* (Job. 9:4); the prophets continually insist that "the *mouth* of the Lord has spoken"; and the historians of Israel never tire of describing what God has done by "thy mighty *hand,* and . . . thy outstretched *arm"* (1 Kings 8:42). Obviously none of this means that for our authors, God has physical and concrete eyes and ears or hands and feet. Like the zones themselves when applied to man, the physical and concrete bodily organ stands symbolically for a sphere and style of human ability and interaction. And when these zones are applied to describe God, the difference between God and man is notably underscored. Everything about God is simply beyond man, including God's concern for his own. As Paul puts it in a hymn he cites: "What no *eye* has seen, nor *ear* heard, nor the *heart* of man conceived, what God has *prepared* for those who love him" (1 Cor. 2:9).

The specific way in which the difference between God and man is highlighted is by the fact that in God's behavior, the three zones work in harmony, effectively. What God conceives in His heart and speaks with His mouth is good and effectively takes place. Man is not consistently effective, nor does he evidence harmony between the three zones. Thus relative to God we find: "For he *spoke,* and it *came to be"* (Ps. 33:9); "I, the LORD, have *spoken,* and I will *do* it" (Ezek. 36:36)—no gap between speech and action; "Has he *said,* and will he not *do* it? Or has he *spoken,* and will he not *fulfil* it?" (Num. 3:19). Another major difference between God and man is that God alone knows the human heart: "Man looks on the *outward appearance,* but the LORD looks on the *heart"* (1 Sam. 16:7; and the texts cited above relative to dyadic personality). And of course, God alone makes and acts on a scale that is incomparable. A perusal of Gen. 1—2:4 reveals God, six times, speaking, making, and seeing—the three zones. For example: "God *said,* 'Let there be light'; and there *was* light. And God saw that the light was good . . . God *said,* 'Let there be lights' . . . God *made* the two great lights, . . . And God *saw* that it was good" (Gen. 1:3–4, 14–18). Notice the harmony between what God says, does, and judges or thinks; and notice how effective this harmony of the interrelated zones is. At the close of this passage (Gen. 1:26), man is described as the image and likeness of God, somewhat like God, yet somewhat unlike Him. How? Why? Again, consider the three zones. Man, like God, has a heart that plans, thinks, judges, chooses; speech that expresses what is in the heart; and activity that realizes what the heart has devised and what speech has expressed. Yet man is unlike God, imperfect, since what he plans often never takes effect, what he says often does not agree with what is in his heart, and what he does often turns out ineffective, incomplete. In sum, man experiences discord among the three zones, something typically human. Yet like God, he functions in terms of the three zones.

If you think this description is exaggerated, consider Ben Sirach's retelling of Israel's past: "He gave them authority over everything on earth, He clothed them with *strength* like his own, and made them in his own image. He filled all living things with dread of man, making him master over beasts and birds. He shaped for them a *mouth* and *tongue, eyes* and *ears,* and gave them a *heart* to think with. He filled them with knowledge and understanding and revealed to them good and evil. He put his own *light* in their *hearts* to show them the magnificence of his *works.* He set knowledge before them, he endowed them with the law of life. He established an eternal covenant with them and revealed his judgments to them. Their *eyes* saw his glorious *majesty* and their *ears* heard the glory of his *voice.* He *said* to them, 'Beware of all wrongdoing'; he gave each a commandment concerning his neighbor. Their ways are always under his *eye,* they cannot be hidden from his *sight.* Over each nation he has set a governor, but Israel is the Lord's own portion. . . . All their *works* are as the sun to him, and his *eyes* rest constantly on their *ways*" (Ecclesiasticus 17:2–19).

In the New Testament, moreover, we find an interesting application of this three-zone model to God. Without doubt, the cause of this new application was Jesus and the question of Jesus' relationship to God. Jesus referred to God as "Father" and "my Father." There are many texts telling us what the Father does, and in these texts the Father functions like God in terms of three zones. However, there are specific texts that mark off the Father relative to Jesus as Son, and in these texts the Father functions in terms of the eyes-heart zone: He is the Father of lights (James 1:17; 1 John 1:5) who is invisible (1 Tim. 1:17) and inaccessible (1 Tim. 6:16). No one has *seen* the Father (John 6:46). Yet the Father *"sees* in secret" (Matt. 6:18), *knows* our *hearts* (Luke 16:15), *loves* the world (John 3:16), *judges* each one impartially according to his *deeds* (1 Peter 1:17), and the like. "Of that day or that hour no one *knows,* not even the angels in heaven, nor the Son, but only the Father" (Mark 13:32). Relative to God, Jesus "is my *beloved* Son, with whom I am well *pleased"* (Matt. 3:17; 17:5).

Further, relative to God, Jesus as Son is revealer of the Father: "All things have been delivered to me by my Father; and no one *knows* the Son except the Father, and no one *knows* the Father except the Son" (Matt. 11:27). This revelation of the Father is described in terms of the mouth-ears function. After all, Jesus is the *Word* of God (John 1:1 ff.); "in these last days he has *spoken* to us by a Son" (Heb. 1:2). "Every one who is of the truth hears my *voice"* (John 18:37). What the Father wants of men is that they heed Jesus, *"listen* to him" (Matt. 17:5). As resurrected Lord, Jesus' command is that his disciples *teach* others to *observe* "all that I have *commanded* you" (Matt. 28:20), in sum, a word that is to be realized. However, note that as man, Jesus manifested three zones like every other man. The Gospels present "all that Jesus began to *do* and *teach"* (Acts 1:1) and often reveal dimensions of his heart ("I am gentle and lowly of *heart"* [Matt 11:29]). Thus in terms of the three zones, Jesus is true man; yet in relation to the Father, he is the Son who reveals the Father, the mouth-ears of God.

Finally, the hands-feet zone applied to God invariably alludes to the Spirit of God. The word "spirit" literally means wind, the main observable energy source of the ancient world apart from human and animal power. The wind runs a range from a cool refreshing breeze to a destructive hurricane or tornado. Wind is power, and the holy wind ("holy Spirit") invariably connotes power, activity, doing, effectiveness. Many of the prophets of the Bible assert that "the *hand* of the LORD" was upon them (1 Kings 18:46 = Elijah; 2 Kings 3:15 = Elisha; Isa. 8:11; Ezek. 3:22). The same holds for the inaugurating New Testament prophet, John the Baptist: "For the *hand* of the Lord was with him" (Luke 1:66). Jesus claims to do good for others by the *finger* of God: "But if it is by the *finger* of God that I cast out demons, then the kingdom of God has come upon you" (Luke 11:20). Thanks to God's Spirit, "many signs and wonders were done among the people by the *hands* of the apostles" (Acts 5:12). On Pentecost day, this same Spirit appears in the form of "tongues as of fire," since the effect of his enabling activity was speech (Acts 2:1–4). In first-century physics, wind, water, and fire have the properties of liquids in contemporary perception. So, like water, wind and fire can be "poured out" (the Latin root word for "pour out over" is "infuse," as the Latin root word for "blow out over" is "inspire"). Hence the Spirit of God can be poured out on all men (Acts 2:17), and water can symbolize the outpouring of the Spirit in baptism. This sort of "poured out over" Spirit can subsequently permeate the hearts and mouths of men, that is, influence all the zones of man, not only man's hands and feet. So the persecuted Christian can "say whatever is given you in that hour, for it is not you who speak, but the Holy Spirit" (Mark 13:11). And the charisms effected by the Spirit in 1 Cor. 12 are all mouth-ears and hands-feet charisms; beyond them lies *agape,* which is an eyes-heart quality (1 Cor. 13).

In sum, it would seem that the distinctive Christian conception of God in terms of the Trinity has its roots in the three-zone model of man typical of the culture we are considering. It is a sort of replication—the application of the same pattern to another area—of the model of man's makeup applied to experiences of God due to the experience of Jesus. Further, the conceptions of God in the Bible in general are likewise rooted in the three-zone model of man.

Summary

According to the perceptions of the group of foreigners we are studying in our New Testament texts, it would seem that a meaningful human existence depends upon an individual's full awareness of what others think and feel about him, and his living up to that awareness. Conscience is sensitivity to what others think about and expect of the individual; it is another word for shame in the positive sense (just like mind is another word for heart). As a result, the person in question does not think of himself or herself as an individual who acts alone regardless of what others think and say. Rather, the person is ever aware of the expectations, of others, especially significant others, and strives to match those expectations. This is the dyadic personality, one who needs another simply to know who he or she is.

Since dyadic personality derives its information from outside of the self and, in turn, serves as a source of outside information for others, anything unique that goes on inside of a person is filtered out of attention. Individual psychology, individual uniqueness, and individual self-consciousness are simply dismissed as uninteresting and unimportant. Instead, all motivations, motives, and attitudes derive from culturally shared stereotypes, from generalities perceived to inhere in certain groups, ranging from one's family to one's village or city to one's nation. These stereotypes, too, derive not from psychological considerations of an individualistic type, but rather from obvious and apparent group traits and behavior. People spend much of their concern on their honor rating within significant groups and in assessing the honor rating of their group relative to others.

Just as society consists of a number of interpenetrating and yet distinct groups comprised of interpenetrating and yet distinct individuals, so too the individual is perceived to consist of interpenetrating yet distinct zones of activity. The existence and function of these zones is verified and validated on the basis of outside, external, concrete observations chunked in terms of three areas: eyes-heart, mouth-ears, and hands-feet. In more abstract terms, eyes-heart is the zone of emotion-fused thought; mouth-ears is the zone of self-expressive speech; and hands-feet is the zone of purposeful activity. Just as individuals act in terms of these three zones, so do groups.

This cultural model of the makeup of man is applied analogically to God. God, too, gets described in terms of these three zones. In the New Testament, due to the central significance of the experience of Jesus, the three zones of the God-model are further refined in terms of specific activity ascribed to the Father, the Son, and the Spirit.

Testing the Hypotheses

The models of dyadic personality and the three zones of human makeup are hypotheses that have to be tested, and it is up to you to test the models and validate them or disprove them.

To test out the dyadic personality model, you might begin by looking up reasons or motivations for behavior presented in the New Testament. An easy way to do this is to look up the conjunctions "for" and "because" in a concordance, then look up the passages and collect those that provide explanation for some line of behavior. For example, here is a sampling of statements containing the Greek conjunction *gar*, meaning "For, because"; it normally sets out a reason for the previous statement. This conjunction is found in all of the following passages, even though your Bible translation might have left it out at times:

Matt. 1:20, 21; 2:2, 5, 6, 13, 20; 3:2, 3, 9, 15; 4:6, 10, 17, 18; 5:12, 18, 20, 29, 30, 46; 6:7, 8, 16, 21, 24, 32, 34; 7:2, 8, 12, 25, 29; 8:9; 9:5, 13, 16, 21, 24; 10:10, 17, 19, 20, 23, 26, 35; 11:13, 18, 30; 12:8, 33, 34, 37, 40, 50; 13:12, 15; 14:3, 4, 24; 15:2, 4, 19, 27; 16:2, 3, 25, 26, 27; 17:15, 20; 18:7, 10, 20; 19:12, 14, 22; 20:1; 21:26, 32; 22:14, 16, 28, 30; 23:3, 5, 8, 9, 13, 17, 19, 39; 24:5, 6, 7, 21, 24, 27, 37, 38; 25:3, 14, 29, 35, 42; 26:9, 10, 11, 12, 28, 31, 43, 52, 73; 27:18, 19, 23, 43; 28:2, 5, 6.

1 Cor. 1:11, 17, 18, 19, 21, 26; 2:2, 8, 10, 11, 14, 16; 3:2, 3, 4, 9, 11, 13, 17, 19, 21; 4:4, 7, 9, 15, 20; 5:3, 7, 12; 6:16, 20; 7:7, 9, 14, 16, 22, 31; 8:5, 10, 11; 9:2, 9, 10, 15, 16, 17, 19; 10:1, 4, 5, 17, 26, 29; 11:5, 6, 7, 8, 9, 12, 18, 19, 21, 22, 23, 26, 29; 12:8, 12, 13, 14; 13:9, 12; 14:2, 8, 9, 14, 17, 31, 33, 34, 35; 15:3, 9, 16, 21, 22, 25, 27, 32, 34, 41, 52, 53; 16:5, 7, 9, 10, 11, 18.

What did the sampling indicate? Are all the reasons stereotypical like proverbs, shared maxims, and/or external, outward, and culturally expected? Or did you find some reasons that are introspective, psychologically unique, extremely personal, and unrepeatable in terms of the culture?

Another useful word to look up in a concordance is the word "know" or "recognize" as applied to persons. On what basis do people get to know one another? How many times are persons said to "know" something about others even though they have never met them?

To test out the three-zone model, look up the main words of the model in a concordance (i.e., eyes, heart, mouth, ears, hands, feet, or any of the other words listed in the text). Then check out how the words are used, singly or in conjunction with others, in the passages you found. Does the model make sense of the texts?

Again, another way to test out both models is to stick to one New Testament writing. This time, take the Gospel of Matthew with the purpose of picking out and explaining dyadic personality and three-zone human makeup. For example:

—Matthew has a large number of Old Testament texts applied to explain behavior, e.g., 1:22; 2:5, 15, 17, 23; 3:3; 4:14; 8:17; 11:10; 12:17, 39; 13:35; 15:7–9; 21:4, 16, 42; 26:56. How would the dyadic personality model explain the use of these texts? Are they stereotypical, unchanging statements from a collection of unchanging words (the Old Testament) applied externally and outwardly to explain a situation, thus indicating it was expected anyway?

—In the temptation story of Matt. 4:1–11, which zones enter the interaction? What sorts of motives are adduced?

—In the call of the Apostles in Matt. 4:18–22, is there any "psychology" of vocation? By what social roles or ranks are those called described? Why—in terms of dyadic personality?

—Note the structure of the final section of the Sermon on the Mount in Matt. 6:19—7:27. Does the first part (Matt. 6:19—7:6) deal with eyes-heart; the second (Matt. 7:7–11) with mouth-ears; and the third (Matt. 7:13–27) with hands-feet?

—Following the Sermon on the Mount, there are ten healings in Matt. 8—9:32. What is said of the psychological state of the sick? Of Jesus? Is each of the sick persons described in terms of personal, unique name and qualities, or in terms of stereotypical, external, outward social categories?

—In terms of dyadic personality, a person's ego-image is shaped by members of his significant group. Who is to shape one's ego image according to Matt. 10:34–39? What of Matt. 12:48–50?

—"For out of the abundance of the heart the mouth speaks" (Matt. 12:34). What does this statement say of the relationship of the three zones? How is this culturally obvious principle applied in Matt. 12:35–37?

—What does Matt. 13:16–17 mean in terms of the three zones?

—In the interpretation of the parable of the sower in Matt. 13:18–23, what is the interaction of the three zones?

—How do people attempt to situate Jesus in Matt. 13:53–57?

—How do the three zones figure in the discussion of clean and unclean in Matt. 15:1–20?

—The "evil eye" in Matt. 20:15 means envy. Why?

—In terms of dyadic personality, what is the meaning of the mother asking for her sons, and the others getting indignant in Matt. 20:20–28?

—According to Matt. 21:28–32, what is more important, mouth-ears or hands-feet? Why?

Let us turn to Paul. Briefly, what is the meaning of "conscience" in the following passages: Rom. 2:15; 9:1; 13:5; 1 Cor. 8:7, 10, 12; 10:25, 27, 28, 29; 2 Cor. 1:12; 4:2; 5:11 (you might also consider 1 Tim. 1:5, 19; 3:9; 4:2; 2 Tim. 1:3; Titus 1:15; Heb. 9:9, 14; 10:22; 13:18; 1 Peter 3:16, 21). Does conscience mean the pain one feels within oneself over some past specific action the individual himself judges to be bad because it was wrong (this is our use of the term)? Or does it mean sensitivity to what others think about and expect of the individual, pain one feels because others consider one's actions inappropriate and dishonorable (this is the dyadic personality use of the term)? Is there sufficient information in these texts to distinguish? Can the model fill in the gaps?

Finally, in 1 Cor. 4:11–13; 2 Cor. 6:4–10; 2 Cor. 11:23–29, Paul presents the culturally well-known "catalog of difficulties"; in terms of dyadic personality, he would be looking for the approval or commendation of his significant others. Is this what is going on in these texts?

4

The Perception of Limited Good

The group of foreigners that we eavesdrop on as we read the New Testament writings comes from the first-century Mediterranean world. What is typical of the first-century Mediterranean world is that it is a nearly perfect example of what anthropologists call classic peasant society: a set of villages socially bound up with preindustrial cities. To understand our foreigners and their concern with honor and shame, it is important to formulate some adequate model of peasant society and the types of perceptions such a society generates.

The Preindustrial City

The basic human environment into which first-century Mediterranean persons—Jews, Romans, Greeks, or otherwise—were born was composed predominantly of agricultural and/or fishing villages socially tied to preindustrial cities. The preindustrial city in question usually served as the administrative, religious, and market center for the villages or towns under its symbolic power. Jerusalem, Corinth, Ephesus, and even Athens and Rome were typical preindustrial cities at this time. The only difference between Rome and the other cities of the area was that Rome served as *the* central city, the imperial hub, to which all other cities were politically tied, while each city individually had a larger or smaller number of villages or towns under its sway. What resulted from this arrangement was a complex of inward looking, closed systems that interfaced or touched upon each other: the village system, the city system, the empire system, and above all of these, the cosmic system.

If you want to imagine what I am talking about, think of the usual Tinkertoy-like model of a molecule composed of connected atoms. The empire was much like the total molecule, while the villages and preindustrial cities to which the villages were socially attached were like atoms, closed circles in which people faced inward, for the most part. Yet each unit of the empire—cities and villages—stands in relation to some other unit that can and does influence its attached surrounding units. What happens in a village can sometimes influence the city, while what happens in the city always influences the connected villages. The influences are not of equal weight. On the other hand, what happens in the imperial city of Rome reverberates throughout the system, while influences from subordinate cities and villages can be brought to bear upon Rome. Consequently, all these human social arrangements called villages, cities, and empire were perceived to be closed and complete within themselves, yet nonetheless related to each other in terms of space (the Mediterranean world), of time (in the first century), and of social interaction (mutual influence among villages, cities, and imperial center). To borrow an expression from biology, this sort of relationship among communities in the Mediterranean world (and peasant societies in general) can be called symbiotic, that is, the living together in more or less close union of two or more dissimilar organisms in a mutually beneficial relationship. In our case we have dissimilar social arrangements in close union that worked to effect mutual benefits, but the larger units always benefited more than the smaller, to be sure. Rome was *the* city, with the rest of the Mediterranean world its surrounding tenancy holdings, its suburbs, if you will. Yet for the Jewish towns and villages of Palestine, Jerusalem was *the* city, with the rest of the country much like its tenancy holdings.

What was life like in the preindustrial city? A city like Jerusalem depended on food, supplies, and raw materials from the outside for its existence. Revelation 18:11–13 offers a list of what was normally imported for this religious and administrative center: "gold, silver, jewels and pearls, fine linen, purple, silk and scarlet, all kinds of scented wood, all articles of ivory, all articles of costly wood, bronze, iron and marble, cinnamon, spice, incense, myrrh, frankincense, wine, oil, fine flour and wheat, cattle and sheep, horses and chariots, and slaves." The city, then, was a market center. And if we cross off the exotic imports, Jerusalem would depend upon the villages of Palestine for wine, oil, flour, wheat, cattle, sheep, cloth, fish, and the like.

The preindustrial city contained no more than ten percent of the entire population under its direct and immediate control. And of this ten percent that constituted the preindustrial urban population, perhaps less than two percent belonged to the elite or high class. The city itself was characterized by rigid social segregation marked by quarters or wards, through which ran streets which were no more than mere passageways for people and for animals used in transportation. The majority of the urbanites (the remaining eight percent) were engaged in handicraft manufacturing, for the most part, and clustered in guilds which inhabited their own sections of the city. The urban house was the workplace, and the producer sold directly to his customer.

In their city section, the small merchants or craftsmen, the day laborers or teamsters, were not much different from the villagers, since the life of the urban elite was normally quite closed off from that of the low-class urbanite. The preindustrial city had no middle class at all. On the other hand, below the low-class urbanite stood the marginal group of beggars and slaves.

The elite or high class of the preindustrial city consisted of literate individuals who held positions in the administrative and religious institutions of the society, along with the wealthy absentee landlords who resided in the city. In the New Testament, the Sadducees and Herodians would normally have belonged to Jerusalem's elite. The members of the city's elite get their status through birth; they belong to the right families, and thus enjoy power, property, and certain highly valued personal attributes, with their position legitimated by the Old Testament writings, for the most part. This is quite clear for the priestly Sadducees, while the princely Herodians would get their legitimation from the sacred writings of the Romans: Roman law, with the Roman prefect in the country to enforce it.

For our purposes, perhaps the most important role of the elite is the fact that they are the bearers of the culture's "Great Tradition," the embodiment of the norms and values which give continuity and substance to the ideals of Jewish society. To find the ideal forms of social norms (marriage, education, religion, government, economics) most closely approximated in reality, we would have to look to the urban literate elite, since they were best able to fulfill the exacting requirements of the sacred writings. This, again, should be obvious for Israel's Temple clergy, their scribes, and the wealthy of the city. As bearers of the Great Tradition, the urban elite had political control, with two principal functions: exacting taxes (especially for the Temple and its city) and maintaining order through a "police force" and a court system which supported the order spelled out by the rules of sacred Scripture, the Torah, which was the law of Israel.

The reason for my describing the preindustrial city, even if so briefly, is that peasant society (the remaining ninety-eight percent of the population consisting of urban non-elites and villagers) is a sort of replication of the preindustrial city elite and stands in symbiotic social relationship to it. The movement set under way by Jesus of Nazareth, as we read about it in the Synoptic Gospels, is essentially a village movement, a movement running through the countryside. Eventually, according to Matthew, Mark, and Luke, Jesus does come to the preindustrial religious and administrative city of Jerusalem. The city elites perceive a threat in this movement, and they annihilate its central symbolic figure. On the other hand, after Jesus' resurrection, the Christian movement gradually makes its way throughout the Mediterranean world as a city movement, from Jerusalem through the cities of the empire to Rome itself. Yet as we see from Paul, even in its preindustrial city expression, the Christian movement does not make any great impact on the city elites.

Hence, by and large, in reading the New Testament we deal with peasant communities in the Synoptics and with non-elite, preindustrial urban communities in Paul and the writings of the Pauline school. From what has been said previously, we might model the populations of the first-century Mediterranean world in terms of four categories: the elites, the urban non-elites, the villagers, and the marginal class. Christianity seems to move within the middle two categories: the urban non-elites and the villagers. What these two groups have in common is that they are the bearers of the culture's "Little Tradition," that is, a simplified and often outdated expression of the norms and ideals embodied by the city elites. To quantify the difference somewhat, we might say that the urban non-elites are usually once or twice removed from "where it's at," while the villagers are two or three times removed from "where it's at," "it" being the lifestyle, norms, and values held by the Great Tradition of the urban elites. What this means for our New Testament documents is that urban elites like the Sadducees, Herodians, and Jerusalemite scribes who belonged to the Sanhedrin would be where "it" was at—the closest approximations of the ideals and values of Jewish society. The non-elite Jerusalemites would be somewhat removed in practice and understanding from the elite expression of the Great Tradition, yet feel capable of mediating that tradition to the countryside at large, to the world at large—and this is where the Jerusalem Pharisees would fit in. On the other hand, Palestinian villagers would be several times removed from the city expression of the ideals and values of Jewish society, living them out in antiquated and often "incorrect" and incomplete form when measured by the urban elite norm. For example, the Galilean Zealot movement could model itself on the outdated aspirations of the Maccabees of the past (about 170 B.C.), while Jesus could very easily be perceived as a prophet of old—something quite passé in urban circles.

There is no such thing as a "grass roots" movement in peasant societies. Villagers and, to a lesser extent, urban non-elites, are what they are (peasants) precisely because they draw upon and develop their cultural forms by imitating customs and values of other, more highly placed members of their wider society. Since these lower-class imitators imperfectly comprehend what they see and hear about city elites, what they acquire from urbanite elites gets reworked, simplified, and cut down so that these elements can be made to fit the less complex arrangements of village or non-elite existence. Normally, by the time novel urban elements are successfully incorporated into non-elite and eventually village culture, urban elite life has changed and moved on, hence villagers always appear old-fashioned to urbanites, while urban non-elites seem behind the times to urban elites.

What this model implies for Bible reading is that the Sadducees, Herodians, and their scribes ought to be imagined as the urban elite trend-setters. Jerusalemite Pharisees and their scribes would belong to the urban non-elite, with their rural expression in the Pharisee villages. The Zealot or guerrilla movement would be typical of ordinary village life, as would the Palestinian movement set under way by Jesus.

Limited Good: A Basic Cue of Perception

Given the symbiotic social arrangement between village and preindustrial city, along with the sectional and segmented structure of the preindustrial city itself, the overwhelming majority of persons living in the first-century world (about ninety-eight percent, as we have said) would find themselves subject to the demands and sanctions of power-holders outside their social realm. Their lot was an unquestioned, if uneasy, acceptance of dominance by some supreme and remote power, with little control over conditions that governed their lives. This means that for the most part (exceptions will be listed below), the people presented in the pages of the New Testament would see their existence as determined and limited by the natural and social resources of their village, their preindustrial city, their immediate area and world, both vertically and horizontally. Such socially limited and determined existence could be verified by experience and lead to the perception that all goods available to a person are, in fact, limited. Thus broad areas of behavior are patterned in such a way as to suggest that such persons believe that in their social, economic, and natural universes—their total environment—all the desired things in life, such as land, wealth, prestige, blood, health, semen, friendship and love, manliness, honor, respect and status, power and influence, security and safety—literally all goods in life—exist in finite, limited quantity and are always in short supply.

Further, not only is it obvious that all conceivable good things in life are finite in number and limited in quantity, but it is equally apparent that there is no way directly within a person's power to increase the available quantities. It is much as though the obvious fact of land shortage and/or housing opportunity in a densely populated area applied to all other desired things in life: simply not enough to go around. The good things constituting life, like land itself, are seen as inherent in nature, there to be divided and redivided, if possible and necessary, but never to be increased.

Since all good exists in limited amounts which cannot be increased or expanded, it follows that an individual, alone or with his family, can improve his social position only at the expense of others. Hence any apparent relative improvement in someone's position with respect to any good in life is viewed as a threat to the entire community. Obviously, someone is being deprived and denied something that is his, whether he knows it or not. And since there is often uncertainty as to who is losing—it may be me and my family—any significant improvement is perceived not simply as a threat to other single individuals or families alone, but as a threat to all individuals and families within the community, be it village or city quarter.

It should not be too difficult for you to imagine what the perception of limited good is like, given the present oil shortage and the recent problem in gasoline distribution. Gasoline would be a limited good: there is only so much to go around. How do you feel when someone at the back of the line moves in ahead of you? How do other folks in line feel about line-jumpers? Are you willing to give up your car or air conditioner so that there might be more oil to go around, or do you think you might be cheated of your fair share, since others won't give up their oil guzzlers? Our basic cultural difficulty with the oil shortage is that we believe all goods are limitless, hence it must be profit-hungry oil companies and middlemen who create shortages to their benefit. To understand our first-century group of foreigners, however, take your experience of gasoline shortage and apply it to all the good things, persons, relationships and events of your life; imagine them to be in short supply at all times, just like gasoline. How would you maintain your standard of living, your self-image that so frequently depends on that standard of living in our society? Could you get ahead without making enemies? What or who would there be to help you out when you are faced with a need?

To return to the first century and its perception of all goods in life as limited, within the limited and finite social arrangements of the village or city section, community stability and harmony among individuals and families can develop and be maintained only by keeping to the existing arrangements of statuses. Thus most people would be interested in maintaining things just the way they are. The honorable man would be greatly concerned about maintaining stability and harmony; he is much interested in preserving his inherited status. Now what the honorable man does is work at preserving his status in two chief ways: (1) by using a sort of personal defensive strategy toward others with whom he does not want to get involved and (2) by striking up selective dyadic alliances with those with whom he does want to get involved. We shall now consider each of these approaches and their implications for the New Testament.

The Honorable Man's Defensive Strategy

Status refers to a person's social position relative to other human beings in the same social system. We reveal our status by the social roles we play—the way we act, feel, and think. These roles, abstractly considered, consist of rights and obligations, the rights we believe we have in our interactions with others, and the obligations others have toward us in respecting our rights. Naturally, we have a corresponding obligation to acknowledge the rights of others. Status in the first-century Mediterranean world derives mainly from birth and is symboled by the honor and prestige already accumulated and preserved by one's family. The honorable man, the first-century ideal, is one who knows how to live out and live up to his inherited obligations. He neither encroaches upon others nor allows himself to be exploited or challenged by others. He works to feed and clothe his family. He fulfils his community and ceremonial obligations. He minds his own business in such a way as to be sure no one else infringes upon him, while looking for possible advantages for himself. In sum, he does not seem to be outstanding, but he knows how to protect his rights to his inherited status.

Moreover, the honorable man feels he has a right to fulfill his inherited role, hence a right to economic and social subsistence. The right to subsistence—to the preservation of one's status in all the dimensions of the ideal man's role—is the active moral principle in peasant societies. In other words, the only time our first-century villager or non-elite urbanite will rebel is when his subsistence is taken away. And should this happen, rebellion is not for the purpose of achieving some higher standard of living or some new social status, but only to return to normal subsistence levels. For example, it was the perception of loss of subsistence due to Roman fixed percentage taxation that spawned the Galilean guerrilla movement known as the Zealots. (The Roman name for a guerrilla of this kind was "thief"; Barabbas was one of these guerrillas, and Jesus was crucified between two such "thieves.")

For our ideal first-century man, what was basic to human living itself was the maintenance and defense of one's valuable self-image, one's honor. To deprive a person of honor in word and/or deed is what the Jewish vocabulary for interpersonal sin is about, as we have previously seen. Given the foregoing abstract description of the honorable man in limited-good society, how did he behave at a more concrete level?

To demonstrate to his fellows that he does not in fact encroach upon their good, the ideal man maintains a culturally predictable, transparent, socially open existence. What this means is that he lives in a way that allows others to know what he is up to. Being a dyadic personality, he himself needs feedback from others as well. One way of showing this openness, to reveal that he is no threat to others, is to allow children to roam freely in and out of his house, workplace, or any other situation that might harbor a secret threat to others. Children serve as village or neighborhood communication links. To be hostile to children means to wish to pull something over on others, to intend to close the shutters of one's existence on others. (Note the ready availability of children in the village settings of Matt. 18:2; Mark 9:36; Luke 9:47.) Another form of signaling such openness—giving others the opportunity to check up on one—is to keep the door to one's courtyard and/or house open when the village or neighborhood is up and about. (Note the Gospel scenes of people parading through houses where Jesus is present, e.g., Mark 2:15–16; 7:24b; Matt. 26:6–7.) The honorable man leads a defensive existence. He avoids the appearance of presuming on others, lest such presumption be interpreted as trying to take something that belongs to another. (Note Jesus' response to one who wants him to intervene in a family matter: "Man, who made me a judge or divider over you?" [Luke 12:14].) In other words, the honorable man, the "good" man, embodies a sort of cultural humility which indicates that he seeks nothing that might even remotely belong to another. Thus John the Baptist predictably proclaims his unworthiness in Mark 1:7 (see also Acts 13:25). A person hoping for some benefaction likewise expresses characteristic unworthiness, whether he in fact is or is not worthy (Matt. 8:8; see also Matt. 10:37–38; 22:8; Luke 15:19,21). This point of view moves the honorable man to refuse to give credit to his fellows for anything in his life, for to admit borrowing from others is to confess that one has taken something not rightfully his, that he is consciously upsetting the community balance and the honorable self-image he tries so hard to maintain (see Mark 9:38–40 and perhaps Gal. 1:12 ff.—Paul's protest of being indebted to no man). It is because of perceived community imbalance that "a prophet is not without honor, except in his own country, and among his own kin, and in his own house" (Mark 6:4), that is, within his closed society. The closed community has ready arguments for rejecting an achiever (see Matt. 11:19; Luke 7:34).

Further, the honorable man never admits to initiating bonds or alliances with others; such things either "just happen" or he is "asked by another." He fears that the admission of asking someone who is not somehow already indebted to him may be interpreted as presuming or imposing on another, trying to get something to which he may not be entitled. For example, day laborers have to be "asked" to work and do not seek a job; after all, they have their honor, too (Matt. 20:7: "no one has hired us" in the parable of the vineyard). People become Jesus' disciples because he asks them (Mark 1:17,20; 2:14; 10:21). No one seeks out Jesus for discipleship, since that would be presumptuous and require a put-down (perhaps Luke 9:57–58, 61–62 were originally such put-downs). The same holds for the growth of the Christian movement; people have to be asked, so some have to be sent (Mark 6:7–11; Matt. 10:7–16; Luke 10:1–12); Rom. 10:15). In this vein, note the many summary statements in the Gospels pointing to how people come to Jesus, seeking him out for healing and help, which he does not volunteer without being asked (e.g., Mark 1:32–33, 45b; 3:7–8, etc.). Finally, the honorable man never compliments his fellows or expresses gratitude. If a compliment is given, there is denial that there is any reason for compliment. For the person who compliments is guilty of aggression, of a negative challenge. He is telling someone to his face that he is rising above the dead level that spells security for all, and he is suggesting that he may be confronted with sanctions. The denial of compliments given is the denial of cause for anyone to envy the one complimented. For example, when a man comes up to Jesus and says "Good Teacher, what must I do to inherit eternal life?" Jesus repudiates the compliment, as any honorable man would: "Why do you call me good? No one is good but God alone" (Mark 10:17–18).

Furthermore, to express gratitude after some positive interaction means to call a halt to an initiated, open-ended, reciprocal relationship. A heartfelt "thank you" signifies that our relationship of mutual obligation is closed and finished, since I cannot and will not repay you. Among equals, such "gratitude" is shameful, but with superiors it is honorable, provided that no more interactions with the same superior are foreseen or expected. Thus most people in the Gospels do not thank Jesus after he heals them; rather they praise God from whom good health comes, further implying that they might have to interact with Jesus again should illness strike later (see Mark 2:12; Matt. 9:8; 15:31; Luke 5:26; 7:16; 13:13; 18:43; 19:37; Gal. 1:24). To thank Jesus would mean that the relationship is over (e.g., Luke 17:16—the Samaritan thanks Jesus).

So much for the honorable man's personal defensive strategy. Now let us consider the type of dyadic alliances he might use with those with whom he intends to get involved.

The Honorable Man's Dyadic Alliances

With his perception of all good as limited, our first-century man of honor found that hard work, thrift with a view to future acquisition, and personal skills and abilities were human qualities quite necessary for maintaining one's status, but useless for getting ahead. Given the limitations on land and resources, along with the lack in inanimate sorts of energy to power technology, additional hard work, development of one's abilities and skills, or achieving goals simply did not produce any significant gain in wealth or influence, in power or broader loyalty. In a village where farms and shops are small, as well as in a preindustrial city where family industry is limited, wealth is accumulated extremely slowly, if at all. There are few ways, if any, for a landless tenant farmer to become a smallholder, for a smallholder to become a large landowner, for a petty shopkeeper, merchant, or craftsman to become wealthy of and by himself within his limited social environment. Now if to move beyond one's limited share in life would lead to challenges and reprisals of all sorts, how is an honorable person in need, in trouble or in dire straits to find rescue from his difficult situation? In the common Greek of the first century, "salvation" meant rescue from a difficult situation; it was not a specifically God-oriented word, but rather much like our word "redemption" when used of trading stamps. Our first-century man of honor was certainly interested in salvation in a whole range of forms, depending upon the need that befell him and his family. Where would he look for salvation if crops failed, if a family member took ill, if bride-wealth was needed for a marriage, if taxes proved too high? The culture provided him with a traditional but limited form of cooperation with both his village peers and with outsiders of equal or higher standing.

Perhaps the most significant form of social interaction in the limited-good world of the first century is an informal principle of reciprocity, a sort of implicit, non-legal contractual obligation, unenforcable by any authority apart from one's sense of honor and shame. By means of this principle of reciprocity, the honorable man selects (or is selected by) another for a series of ongoing, unspecified acts of mutual support. This is what George Foster calls the "dyadic contract." He defines it as an implicit contract informally binding pairs of contractants rather than groups (recall that dyad means a pair, a twosome). In our limited-good world, such contracts can bind persons of equal status (colleague contracts) or persons of different statuses (patron-client contracts). These informal contracts function side by side with the formal contracts of society like buying and selling, marriage, the natural covenant with God, and the like. However, the dyadic contract cross-cuts the formal contracts of the culture, serving as the glue that holds individuals together for long or short terms, and enabling the social interdependence necessary for life.

Dyadic contracts are initiated by means of the positive challenges we spoke of previously. For example, the acceptance of an invitation to supper, of a small gift, or of a benefaction like healing was equivalent to a positive challenge requiring a response. It signaled the start of an ongoing reciprocal relationship. To accept an invitation, a gift, or a benefaction with no thought to future reciprocity implies acceptance of imbalance in society. Such an action would damage the status quo. Within a closed system, this does not happen without grave repercussions, for in reality there are no free gifts, just gifts which mark the initiation or continuance of an ongoing reciprocal relationship. Thus in Luke 5:27–32, Jesus invites Levi, a toll collector, to follow him. Levi accepts and then reciprocates by inviting Jesus to a feast with his friends. Each invitation is a positive challenge, a gift that requires repayment. Such positive challenges and appropriate responses will continue indefinitely, embracing a range of goods and services, provided that an exactly even balance between two partners is never struck. It is this sort of dyadic contractual relationship that bothers Jesus' critics when he eats with "sinners and tax collectors" (see also Mark 2:15–16; Matt. 11:19). Now if a balance in reciprocity were struck, or if one's partner called a halt to responding with a verbal display of gratitude, that would signify the end of the ongoing reciprocity. This sort of reciprocity among equals is a symmetrical one between closely located persons of the same social status, hence a colleague contract.

I might mention, by the way, that even buying and selling involved reciprocal obligations of a symmetrical sort, for in the context of limited good, the seller always does the buyer a favor by selling to him. It is always a seller's market. Thus, even if an entire village consists of the same sort of producers (e.g., fishermen), or an entire preindustrial city quarter contains artisans producing the same merchandise, all are assured of their clientele because of previous dealings with them; hence such small merchants are not in competition with each other, as they would be in our society.

A patron-client contract, on the other hand, is very similar to a colleague contract in that it is initiated by means of a positive challenge, a positive gift. But it ties persons of significantly different social statuses, hence the goods and services in the ongoing reciprocal relationship will be different. The relationship is asymmetrical since the partners are not social equals and make no pretense to equality. We might say that with equals in colleague contracts, a man provides himself with all he needs, at peak periods of demand, of the kinds of goods and services to which he himself also has access. The patron-client contract, on the other hand, provides things not normally available in the village or urban neighborhood, things that at times are badly needed. Both sorts of relationship require imbalance for continuance, and both can be discontinued with varying degrees of sanction.

Patron-client relationships seem to be implied in the Gospels when people approach Jesus for "mercy" (e.g., Matt. 9:27—blind men; 15:22—Canaanite woman; 17:15—father of an epileptic; 20:30—blind men again). Furthermore, all positive relationships with God are rooted in the perception of patron-client contracts. For example, the charisms listed by Paul in 1 Cor. 12 and Rom. 12 are gifts from God naturally requiring repayment in the forms of loyalty, obedience, honor, and submission. Such gifts coming from the patron, God, look to long-term continuance. However, there are forms of patron-client contracts of a shorter term, of a non-continuing kind. For example, vows to God like the Nazirite vow Paul made (Acts 18:18; see Acts 21:23–24 for others, and Num. 6:1–21 for the rules) are such short-term contracts. Once the patron, God, grants the request and the client complies by fulfilling his vow, a balance is struck and the relationship for this purpose is terminated.

All in all, our first-century foreigners made their way through life by attempting to strike up dyadic contracts that they felt might be helpful. Over time, a person would build contractual relationships with fellow villagers and friends in other communities, occasionally dropping those that no longer served and developing new ones that offered promise. Every person worked out or tried to work out similar ties with more powerful persons, with human and non-human patrons. Their approach was pragmatic and eclectic, based on trial and error, and in a spirit of "nothing ventured, nothing gained." Thus an honorable man looked for ways to interest and obligate potential partners whom he felt could help him, and in so doing committed himself to carry out the terms of the contract with those who, in effect, accepted his offer. By means of a greater or lesser number of such contractual ties with both peers and superiors, the typical person of the first-century Mediterranean world maximized his interests and security posture in the uncertain world in which he lived.

From the viewpoint of the dyadic contract, Jesus' call to others to follow him in the Gospels is an instance of an individual initiating reciprocal relationships with other individuals. At times Jesus meets with a refusal, as in the case of the rich man (Mark 10:17–31; Matt. 19:16–30; Luke 18:18–23). The important thing to note is that the dyadic contract obliges no wider group than the individuals (and perhaps their embedded females and children) who made the contract. Consequently, it would be quite normal for the disciples of Jesus to squabble with and challenge each other, since they have ties to Jesus and not to each other (e.g., Luke 9:46; 22:24). Further, Jesus makes appeals to individuals on a dyadic basis, for example: "Come to me, all who labor and are heavy laden, and I will give you rest" (Matt. 11:28). The teacher-disciple relationship is equally dyadic (Matt. 10:24). Finally, the factions in the church of Corinth seem to have derived from dyadic relationships to individual apostles (1 Cor. 1:12). I might point out here, incidentally, that Paul's solution to the problem posed by such dyadism, much like the solution envisioned in Matt. 23:8–10, is to point out that obligations owed to Jesus have to be paid back not to Jesus, but to others in dyadic relation with Jesus, that is, one's fellow Christians. The result is a sort of polyadic relationship ("poly-" means many): a number of people in equivalent social statuses organized around a single interest and mutually obligated in terms of this single interest, much like a guild or Roman burial association.

Limited Good and the Accumulation of Wealth

How would our honorable first-century foreigner look upon profit-making or the accumulation of wealth? From all that we have considered so far, most people in the first century Mediterranean world worked to maintain their inherited status, not to get rich. The goal of life in a closed society such as theirs is contentment derived from preserving one's status, not acquisition or achievement. With such a goal in mind, it would be impossible to attempt to convince such people that they might improve their social standing with more work. For this reason, you will find no Puritan or Communist work ethic in the New Testament. Nor will you find any program of "social action" aimed at the redistribution of wealth or anything of the sort. The closest thing to this sort of conception in the time of Jesus and Paul would be the Zealot movement. However, like all peasant movements, the Zealots were not after the reshaping of society, but rather the restoration of the subsistence economy to which all peasants believe they have a right.

On the contrary, in the closed type of society we are considering, the honorable person would certainly strive to avoid and prevent the accumulation of capital, since he would see in it a threat to the community and community balance, rather than a precondition to economic and social improvement. Since all goods are limited, one who seeks to accumulate capital is necessarily dishonorable; the operative dirty word in this regard is "greed." A person could not accumulate wealth except through the loss and injury suffered by another. A fourth-century Mediterranean proverb says: "Every rich person is either unjust or the heir of an unjust person." The outlook was the same in the first century.

By and large, only the dishonorable rich, the dishonorable non-elites, and those beyond the pale of public opinion (like city elites, governors, and regional kings) could accumulate wealth with impunity. This they did in a number of ways, notably by trading, tax collecting, and money lending. At bottom, the trader, the tax collector, and the money lender (at interest, of course) were all the same: they made profit by defrauding others, by forcing people to part with their share of limited good through extortion. The money lender could have his debtors imprisoned, the purpose of imprisonment being to put pressure on the debtor's family to pay off the money due (e.g., Matt. 5:25–26; Luke 12:57–59). During the ministry of Jesus, the Romans collected their own taxes in Judea, while the Herodians did so in Galilee. However, there were toll collectors, like Levi, who collected indirect taxes (similar to the taxes we pay on liquor, food, gasoline, that is, sales taxes). In the process, the toll collector would collect as much as he could squeeze from the people over and above what the Romans demanded, then pay his share to the Romans and pocket the rest (e.g., Luke 3:13; 19:1–9). Finally, the trader, the inter-city import-export merchant of the preindustrial city, was often a freedman or urban non-elite person secretly subsidized by wealthy Roman citizens or other elites. Traders bought needed commodities in one place and sold them in another at monopoly prices, getting as much as they could regardless of their own costs. All these forms of capital accumulation were perceived to be forms of usury. Technically, usury means making money on the use of money, much as our banks and other modern lending institutions do; in the first century they would all be considered dishonorable and immoral forms of usury. Trading, in turn, meant making money by investing in some goods purchased abroad with the hope (and certainty) of selling for a much higher price at home (e.g., Luke 19:12–27). The trader, like the money lender and the tax collector, was considered basically godless. For example, in James 4:13–16, traders talk as follows: "Today or tomorrow we will go into such and such a town and spend a year there and trade and get gain." (Read the whole passage. The criticism in the passage is that traders do not trust in God, but in their own devices.)

Thus, in preindustrial societies, profit and gain normally refer to something that accrues to a person by fraud or extortion, that is, something other than wages, customary rent, reciprocal lending, or direct sale from producer to consumer. Paul reminds his readers that "wages are not reckoned as a gift" (Rom. 4:4), yet some wealthy persons would defraud wage-earners by reneging on what they owed (James 5:1–6). Such greed was typical of the "lovers of money," those who sought capital accumulation, a thoroughly dishonorable line of conduct (see 1 Tim. 3:8, 13; 6:5, 6; Titus 1:7, 11; 1 Peter 5:2; 2 Peter 2:15; Jude 1:11, 16; note also Mark 10:19:"Do not defraud"; 1 Cor. 6:7–8; Matt. 20:1–15).

Now the honorable man would not want to be branded as "greedy," hence the accumulation of capital, the pure profit motive, was closed to him. This is typical of a limited-good, closed society with its contentment and status-maintenance orientation. In such a society, the saying "For you always have the poor with you" (Mark 14:7; Matt. 26:11; John 12:8) is a cultural truism, something obvious to any thinking, reasonable person in the first-century Mediterranean world. But there is more to it than meets the eye. For who in fact are the poor in a limited-good society?

In peasant societies, "poor" is not a designation of class or a reference to the lowest class in a series of such classes. As a matter of fact, being "poor" is not primarily an expression of economic rank at all. The culture that we study has its prime focus and pivotal values in honor and shame. The class into which one is born, regardless of how high or low, is normally honorable. Money is not the determiner of class ranking as it is in our society; rather, birth is. Then what does being "poor" refer to? If we consider the data presented in the New Testament, we find two sets of usages of the word. First of all, there is a series of passages in which the word "poor" is used without further description. From such passages we simply cannot get any idea of what the authors are referring to except by sticking our own ideas into their words (e.g., Matt. 19:21; 26:9, 11; Mark 10:21; 14:5, 7; Luke 18:22; John 12:5–8; 13:29; Rom. 15:26; 2 Cor. 6:10; 8:9; 9:9; Gal. 2:10).

On the other hand, there is also a series of passages in which the word "poor" is used in the company of other words that describe the condition of the person who is labeled "poor." Thus, Luke 4:18 has a quote from Isaiah in which the poor are those imprisoned, blind, debt-ridden; Matt. 5:3 ff., along with Luke 6:20–21 have the poor ranked with those who hunger, thirst, and mourn (a mourner is one afflicted with evil who by mourning protests the presence of evil); Matt. 11:4–5 lists the blind, lame, lepers, deaf, and the dead with the poor, while Luke 14: 13, 21 has the maimed, lame, and the blind. Further, Mark 12:42–43 and Luke 21:2–3 speak of a poor widow, and Luke 16:20–22 tells of the poor Lazarus who was full of sores, hence ill, leprous. Finally, James 2:3–6 points out the shabbily dressed poor man as truly powerless, while Rev. 3:17 considers the poor to be wretched, pitiable, blind, naked—something like the list in Matt. 25:34 ff., where we find the hungry, thirsty, stranger, naked, and imprisoned.

Now if we were to take all these adjacent descriptions of the poor and group them in terms of what they have in common, it would seem that being classified as poor was the result of unfortunate personal history or circumstances. A poor person seems to be one who cannot maintain his inherited status due to circumstances that befall him and his family, like debt, being in a foreign land, sickness, death (widow), or some personal physical accident. Consequently, the poor would not be a permanent social class, but a sort of revolving class of people who unfortunately cannot maintain their inherited status. Thus day laborers, landless peasants, and beggars born into such situations are not poor persons in first-century society, and poor would not be an economic designation. Furthermore, the opposite of rich would not necessarily be poor. In the perception of people in limited-good society, the majority of people are neither rich nor poor, just equal in that each has a status to maintain in some honorable way. Personal assessment is not economic, but a matter of lineage. Thus in this context, rich and poor characterize two poles of society, two minority poles—the one based on the ability to maintain elite status, the other based on the inability to maintain one's inherited status of any rank.

Limited Good and Personal Causality

If the ordinary first-century person always had the poor with him, so did he always have the rich—if not in his village or city quarter, then somewhere else, to be sure. As pointed out above, the honorable man would seek out patron-client contracts with those of higher status, especially to provide goods and services not normally available in the village or urban neighborhood. When faced with some abnormal crisis, he would attempt to tap the proper higher class resource in a variety of ways. This could be done far more easily than in our individualistic society, for the higher class person was a dyadic personality as well. He too needed to live up to the ego-image provided by others and sanctioned by public opinion. The client would repay his patron by such intangibles as public praise, concern for his reputation among those of the client's status, informing the patron of plots and machinations of others—in sum, by continually adding to the name and honor of the patron. In the highly stratified, status-conscious social system of the first-century world, elites had a rightful place. The obvious inequality of persons and social classes that we notice was considered normal, useful, and God-given. After all, we do not have control over our family of birth, its status, wealth, and prestige. These we inherit according to God's good pleasure. (You might also consider that social distinction is not discrimination except when your society claims that all men are legally equal. First-century society never made a claim about the legal equality of all men.)

The honorable higher class person, then, like the lower class person, was expected to live out and live up to his socially ascribed self-image. And this entailed the obligation of serving as patron for clients of lower social strata. This arrangement enabled members of any given closed system to seek and often gain access to other systems, for example, the tenant farmer to the landowner, the village artisan to some urbanite, and both of these to some local administrative office holder, to the emperor, to the gods or to God. The centurion of Capernaum, who "built us our synagogue" in Luke 7:1–10, was such an available patron. Paul's appeal to the emperor in Acts 25:25 is an instance of seeking the salvation available to a Roman citizen. From a limited-good perspective, an individual faced with an unusual crisis might achieve a solution to it by tapping sources perceived to stand outside his stratum or system. If such a maneuver succeeds, the success might be envied by one's peers within his closed system, but it is not seen as a direct threat to community stability, for no one within the community loses anything. Still, such success has to be made known publicly and explained to others.

In other words, what needs explanation to prevent community recrimination and reprisal is success found at the boundaries of one's closed system and the system adjacent to it. Positive results from contacts at these boundaries were attributed to luck, good fortune, or Providence. For example, finding a lost sheep or a lost coin (Luke 15:6–9) and the joy accompanying it requires public explanation to prevent suspicion of theft. Male children—an economic asset in most classes of first-century society—are normally ascribed to God (Luke 1:13). Note also the parables of the Kingdom in Matt. 13:44 (treasure in a field); 13:45 (finding a pearl); 13:47–48 (dragnet and fish). In all of these, the situation of the Kingdom is compared to the activity of people who find success due to luck or good fortune. On the otherhand, parables dealing with prayer to patrons of various sorts (for example Luke 18:1–5 [widow and judge]; Matt.7:7–8 [beggar's behavior]; Luke 18:9–14 [God and the Pharisee and publican]; as well as the prayers of various people to Jesus, for example, Mark 10:46–52 [the blind beggar Bartimaeus]; Mark 10:35–41 [the request of James and John]) indicate how one might have recourse to a higher class patron ranging from a local prestigious person to a local king to God.

This last mentioned point is rather significant for understanding a very fundamental cue of perception shared by our group of foreigners. As pointed out many times previously, in limited-good societies, hard work, acquisition of goods, and human abilities simply cannot bring forth the power and commitment needed to rescue a person from an abnormal difficult situation. Another way to say this is that an individual's manipulation of his available world of things, of "its," is simply non-productive and insufficient for adequate rescue from very difficult situations. Such human manipulation of the available world of things is technology, and first-century technology, even if it were applied exhaustively, yielded no significant increase in wealth or influence. Consequently, apart from luck or good fortune, the only source of help would lie in the manipulation of the available world of people, of "thou's," of higher class persons who can provide relief in unusual situations (peers and colleague contracts take care of usual needs). Furthermore, if luck and fortune ultimately derive from God or the gods, then the divinity too becomes a "thou" worthy of manipulation. What I mean is that if in order to make it in life, it is obvious to all that technology, hard work, and technical abilities are all a waste of time and highly threatening to others even if they can be applied, then all that is left for the individual is to learn how to manipulate other individuals to his advantage. Such manipulation requires awareness and skill, since most often the person offering the most good will be one of a higher class. This cultural fact—that success in life derives from manipulating persons—leads to some conclusions typical of the limited-good outlook.

The first conclusion—an important cue of perception—is that every effect that counts in life is caused by a person, so that when something significant happens, positive or negative, the question to ask is "Who did it?" (not "What did it?" as we ask in our culture). It further follows that some persons are more powerful than others, as can readily be proved by the effects caused by various persons. The key to success, then, is to get to know the power of the person with whom an honorable man can actually or potentially interact and to use those persons for one's own ends, for salvation from a difficult situation. Take sickness and pain, for example. In this cultural context, since sickness is something that counts in a person's life, who would cause it? If it is not caused by me or some other human being who might sock, stab, or otherwise hurt me, then it must be caused by some non-human person, a non-human "thou." And if it is person-caused, even by non-human persons, then every healing is in effect wiping out the influence of another person, hence an exorcism—and every exorcism implies a healing.

So the honorable man has to learn how to make it with the persons he comes into contact with, specifically by means of the "sociological" thinking mentioned in the previous chapter. These persons of his social world are both human and non-human. What all this indicates is that in the first-century world, social structures in general (like economics), as well as concrete expressions of those structures (like farming, along with a concrete good harvest or bad, drought, famine, adequate rain, and the like), are perceived as created, maintained, controlled, and governed by various persons, human and non-human, depending on the dimensions of the effects. The parable of the weeds sown in the wheat by an enemy (Matt. 13:24–30) points to a human person. But the grand dimensions of human experience, like weather, life and its transmission, political power, and so on, are far above and beyond any individual human being's control or grasp. These are ascribed to non-human persons. Thus people in our period perceived God, gods, and their agents—spirits, demons, angels—as necessary to maintain the equilibrium both of society and its pursuits in social and physical environments, most often regardless of what men themselves might do. In other words, for the first-century Mediterranean person, nearly all the social realities singled out in our modern textbooks and courses in sociology, social psychology, and the natural sciences would be perceived as "religious" phenomena. The reason for this is that religion dealt with respect for those who controlled human existence, hence the non-human and human persons above us to whom we owe a debt of honor and respect.

Thus the surest and most common sources of help and security available to people of the first-century Mediterranean society were persons of the same rank and especially higher ranking human and non-human beings who controlled their existence to a large extent. The key to success was to learn how to manipulate the available persons. The patron-client contract looks to one phase of this sort of manipulation in the relationship between superiors and subordinates. Our first-century villagers and urban non-elites believed that they had a moral right to subsistence and to reciprocal interaction with the more fortunate elites of their social world, ranging from the local wealthy landowner to the gods or God. So long as these elites allowed the lower classes their subsistence, it did not matter how much they took in taxes, tribute, sacrifice, and the like. And so long as these elites allowed lower classes to interact with them in patron-client relationships, it did not matter how unequal they might be in prestige and power.

Limited Good and the Structured Social World

Before concluding this chapter, we might consider the general structure of the social world experienced by those foreigners whom we study when we read the New Testament. The perception of limited good leads to the perception of personal causality. The dyadic contract was one important way for a person to make his way in a world where what persons caused determined everything important in life. This world of persons consisted of a set of statuses that embraced all of reality, reaching up to the cosmos, with God at the top. Given the obvious principle that to harm or help one person it took another person, human or non-human, the first-century Mediterranean social world would be inhabited by persons standing in vertical relationship to each other and within limited, closed, horizontal systems somewhat as follows:

1) God: On top was God, whom the Mediterranean world knew as "the Most High" (e.g., Luke 1:32, 35; 2:14; 6:35). Semites in general, Israelites in particular, believed that all things are possible with God (e.g., Luke 1:37, Mark 10:27; Matt. 19:26; Luke 18:27). Roman and Greek elites believed that God himself was limited: he could not make a square circle, make rivers run backward, cause the oceans to overrun land, and the like.

2) Gods or sons of God or archangels: These comprised a sort of heavenly bureaucracy doing the bidding of God. Satan (a Persian name for a spy, a secret service agent), or the devil (the Greek translation of Satan), was originally God's secret service agent, as in Job 1; by the first century this negative person leads a sort of palace revolt against God, and in it he likewise involves humans (e.g., see Luke 4:6). Beings at this level can influence everything below them, but not God. They are controlled by God.

3) Lower non-human persons: These include suprahuman forces that faze man's world and are called angels (in origin a Semitic term for a messenger from the heavenly court, a sort of heavenly factotum), spirits (a Semitic term for suprahuman power known by its effects), or demons (the Greek word for such suprahuman powers). These, too, could influence at will everything below them, but not those above them. They got their orders from those above them, ultimately all under God's control.

4) Man: This level comprises the world of men in structured society, running along a scale from emperor to slave for the empire, from high priest to slave in Israel. In this pyramidal structure, persons of higher rank could influence all below them at will, but not vice versa.

5) Beings lower than man: If such creatures affect man, that is due to the manipulation of others up and down this ladder of persons who use them to their own advantage.

Meaningful survival clearly entailed maintaining one's place on this ladder. For his own well-being and security— or simply because that is his nature—each higher type person attempts to manipulate the lower and looks to non-interference from his horizontal colleagues. For a lower ranking person to gain effective influence on some higher being, a patron intermediary is necessary to act as a social lever, a sort of go-between. The patron, of course, must come from the same sphere as the higher being one wishes to influence, or from a sphere above that being. God, being on the top of the status ladder, has all others under effective control.

Summary

The first-century Mediterranean world might be characterized as a peasant society, that is, a society of preindustrial cities along with surrounding villages over which the cities exercise control and influence. The majority of the people of the time lived in villages or in artisan quarters of the preindustrial city. For this majority (and perhaps the minority elite as well), the main perception in life was that all goods are limited. This perception lies behind the behavior considered necessary for an adequate human existence. The basic need for security in a threatening and threatened world, prismed through the image of limited good, revealed the sources of power and influence, of wealth and loyalty, at the interfaces of one's closed system as well as among select members of one's peer group. Behavior at this boundary, horizontally considered, entailed reciprocal obligations with one's colleagues. Vertically considered, such behavior took the shape of the patron-client system. Both colleague relationships and patron-client relationships entailed reciprocal obligations that might be called dyadic contracts.

The honorable man in the world of limited good was one who knew how to preserve his inherited status. In his quest to maintain this important self-image, the honorable man knew how to use his colleagues as well as his powerful and socially superior fellow men and non-human persons to meet life's problems. This, of course, implied the need for knowledge of patrons, a sort of popular political science. The human patron-client system had a comparable non-human system in the beings that controlled human existence, resulting in a cosmic patron-client system that embraced the human as well. So the honorable man also knew how to manipulate the available non-human powerful persons to help in meeting life's problems. This likewise implied a need for knowledge of cosmic patrons, a sort of popular and personalistic natural science along with a knowledge of God.

Testing the Hypothesis

Once again, it is up to you to prove or disprove the models just presented. This time we shall use the Gospel of Luke as a quarry for the data that might validate or invalidate the model. However, I would like to begin with a caution. It seems that the author of the Gospel of Luke did not know Palestine very well in the sense that he ranks as cities (Greek: *polis*) places that certainly were no more than villages, even large villages, e.g., Nazareth and Bethlehem. The main preindustrial cities in Palestine during the period of the New Testament were Jerusalem, Caesarea (where the Roman prefect lived), Tiberias (where Herod Antipas lived), Sebaste and Neapolis in Samaria, and the ten-city league known as the Decapolis (Greek for "ten cities"). And there were some cities along the Mediterranean shore as well. Perhaps Luke calls certain places "cities" to intimate to his readers that the persons coming from those places were elites of sorts, not just country peasants. You might test out this idea by looking up the word "city" in an r.s.v. concordance, taking out the listing for Luke, and checking on who comes from those places and what roles they have in the Gospel story.

To test out the models in this chapter, try the following:

—Based on the hierarchy of classes mentioned throughout the chapter, rank the following in terms of class as presented in the first three chapters of Luke: 1:5: Herod, king of Judea (37–4 B.C.); Zechariah, a priest; Elizabeth, an Aaronite, of priestly family; 1:19, 26: Gabriel (the name of "God's power"), angel of the presence (of God); 1:27: Mary and Joseph of Nazareth, a Galilean village, of low estate (1:48; 2:4–5); 2:1–2: Caesar Augustus (27 B.C.–A.D. 14), Quirinius, governor of Syria; 2:8 ff. shepherds; 2:25: Simeon the Jerusalemite; 2:36: Anna, the Jerusalemite, a widow; 2:46: teachers in the Jerusalem Temple; 3:1: Tiberius Caesar (A.D. 14–37); Pontius Pilate, governor of Judea (A.D. 25–36); Herod Antipas (4 B.C.–A.D. 39); Philip (4 B.C.–A.D. 34: these last two were children of Herod the Great, mentioned in 1:5); Annas and Caiaphas, high priests. If you have the patience, you might try to rank all the persons mentioned in Luke. From the ranking what can you deduce about social interactions?

—In the preaching of John the Baptist (3:10–14), what sort of social reform is involved: a social revolution, sharing the wealth with all, or simply helping people maintain their original status? Who are the greedy, evil ones mentioned here? Why would their calling put them on dubious footing limited-good society?

—In terms of limited good, why did Jesus' fellow townsmen reject him in 4:14–30? Note that in 4:15, Jesus' reputation has already grown to such an extent that he was "glorified" (i.e., held in high, publicly acknowledged honor) by all except the folks of Nazareth.

—Jesus heals Simon's mother-in-law in 4:38–39. Does this explain why Jesus could use Simon's boat in 5:3? Notice that Simon has a colleague contract with James and John in 5:10. According to this passage, what sort of debt do

Simon, James, and John owe Jesus for the catch of fish? Is Jesus much like a patron soliciting clients in a dyadic way?

—Jesus forms a dyadic tie with Levi in 5:27-30. What is Levi's response? Why a meal with his friends? Does the dyadic contract indicate why?

—The passage at 6:1–5 will make more sense if you read the law behind it, namely Deut. 23:24–25. What does this imply about limited good? To whom does the land, the Holy Land, ultimately belong? To whom are people indebted for the fruit of the land?

—Note the implied cultural rules in 6:32-36: "love those who love you"; "do good to those who do good to you"; "lend to those from whom you hope to receive." To carry on a dyadic contract with another is a sign of mutual gratefulness, honor, and friendship. But what is God like, according to Jesus in this passage?

—In 7:1–10, how does the alien centurion get Jesus to come? Note the role of the village elders who act as "levers," gaining a foothold with the wandering teacher (v. 3); then some friends (v. 6) who attest to the fact that the centurion plays a duly humble role, even though he is a higher class foreigner (vv. 6–8).

—If Jesus controlled evil spirits (7:18–23, especially v. 21, and throughout the Gospel), where would you be likely to rank him on the hierarchy or ladder of "persons" listed at the end of this chapter? Who would oppose situating him above the category of men? Or might you list the evil spirits on the human or subhuman level?

—In the parable of the creditor (7:40–42), note the asymmetrical relationship and the degree of debt implied in the patron-client contract. What is the usual behavior toward a guest in one's house in 7:44–46? In the light of the model of patron-client contract, what does it mean to "love much" (v. 47)?

—Why do the wealthy women listed in 8:1–3 provide for Jesus from their means? Does dyadic contract explain why?

—In terms of dyadic contract and honor in limited-good society, how were Jesus' disciples to be supported in 9:1–6; 10:1–12? Why do they have to be sent?

—In the parable of the good Samaritan (10:29–37), what obligation does the man who was helped owe to the Samaritan? In the light of dyadic contract, why would the priest and Levite pass up the injured man?

—How does dyadic contract clarify the parable of the importunate friend in 11:5–8?

—In terms of limited good, what does the parable in 12:16–21 present as typical of a rich man's behavior?

—How does a rich householder deal with his slaves in the light of the parable in 12:42–48? Why?

—In 14:12–14, we have the same cultural rules as those in 6:32–36, and both sets imply dyadic contract. In this context, who is a poor man? Would it be one who cannot carry on a dyadic contract, who is unable to repay or help out another, e.g., the maimed, lame, blind?

—How does the dishonest steward of 16:1–8 firm up dyadic contracts to ensure him his future salvation?

—The story of Zacchaeus the tax (or toll) collector (19:1–8) says he was rich. How did he get rich (v. 8)? What is wrong with getting rich this way in terms of limited good?

—According to 19:12-27, how does the elite nobleman get richer in limited-good culture?

—What is implied in Jesus' certainty that the owner would let him borrow a colt in 19:30–34? Similarly, what of the place for Passover in 22:7–13, and of Joseph of Arimathea, a member of the Jerusalem Sanhedrin (national council) in 23:50–53?

In the light of the models of this chapter, what meaning can you find in Paul's statements about Jesus becoming poor for us, like 2 Cor. 8:9 and the hymn in Phil. 2:6–11?

5

Kinship and Marriage

Up to this point, we have come to know quite a bit about the group of foreigners with whom we interact when we read the New Testament. We can see that their main concerns were lodged within perceptions controlled by honor and shame, in a sort of agonistic arena of life. They participated in this arena of life as dyadic personalities who saw the world as thoroughly limited and controlled by persons of various sorts, a world in which they sought to maintain their inherited status by means of dyadic contractual relationships. The question we turn to now is how they got their inherited status. Obviously, inheritance belongs within the field of family and kinship. What was first-century kinship like? What was the family like, and what did the marriage which constituted the family mean?

In order to answer these sorts of questions, we must once again turn to abstract chunking and model-making, to similarities at a higher level of abstraction in order to see how we and they are similar. At the same time, we will have to dip down into the concrete in order to learn how similarities are expressed quite differently at the level of specific cultural norms and the behavior deriving from those norms.

Kinship

Social norms, as we have seen, present the "oughts" of a group, the cultural cues guiding people to perceive and evaluate the persons, things, and events of their experience. Kinship refers to patterns of such social norms that regulate human relationships which are directly based upon the experiences of birth and the birth cycle, from the womb, through developmental stages, to death. Kinship norms basically fill biological interactions among human beings with meaning and value. In other words, kinship norms symbolize human biological interactions and the ongoing results of such interactions. At bottom, kinship norms are rooted in the social perception that human relationships can be and actually are established among persons by their being born of certain parents or by the possibility of births resulting from the union of two (or more) human beings. Marriage refers to such a union of two (or more) human beings insofar as it relates to kinship; hence marriage is a subset of kinship norms.

The social area covering actual or potential births can be divided into four categories: (1) the selection of marriage partners; (2) the marriage bond—the relatively enduring, socially sanctioned sexual and social union of one or more men with one or more women; (3) the immediate conjugal family of husband(s), wife (wives), and children, i.e., the nuclear family, the family of procreation, and the conjugal family bond; (4) the extended kinship relationship beyond the immediate conjugal family, i.e., the extended family, the family of orientation, and the broader kinship bond. These social categories cover the area of kinship norms and are a form of boundary-marking. For kinship norms make lines between and among people, delineating between "us" and "them" in a regular yet often kaleidoscopic way. Kinship norms indicate as well as regulate and prescribe how closely related one must be in order to be one conjugal family, one extended family, one people. They also point out and control how *other* one must be in order to be a spouse: other sex? other status? other family? other lineage? other nation? They likewise imply a time factor, indicating how long bonds of marriage, family, and extended family stay in force. For example, how long do you expect to be your parents' son or daughter? Does your marriage imply a break in the son/daughter bond, or will that bond continue? What of the brother/sister bond? How long will your parents stay husband and wife? Does this relationship survive death or not? How long must you stay with a partner before others in your group consider you married? Does having a child decide the issue? Why isn't a chance sexual affair the same as a long-term relationship?

Kinship norms, in sum, deal with the selection of marriage partners as well as with the quality and duration of the marriage bond (husband and wife), the conjugal family bond (parents, brothers, sisters = children), and the extended family bond (relatives beyond the immediate conjugal family). The selection of marriage partners, again at a high level of abstraction, derives from how a given culture deals with potentially disruptive conflicts within a kinship group. Internal conflicts, like those caused by the distribution of inheritance and wealth, must be kept within some restricted range. Furthermore, positive cooperation or solidarity has to be maintained at some minimal level, so that the group might survive in a meaningful, human way. The expression of solidarity or positive cooperation can take the form of (1) prohibiting marriages within the kinship unit. This is called exogamy, the requirement that a spouse must come from outside the kinship unit. Exogamy, openness to outside groups, symbols universalism, since it links various solidarity groups on a broader scale (this is the practice in the

United States). Or positive cooperation can take the form of (2) prohibiting marriages outside the kinship group. This is called endogamy, the requirement that a spouse must come from within the kinship unit. Endogamy, closedness to outside groups, symbols particularism, since it results in a society of relatively small, closed segments (this is the preference in the Mediterranean world of the first century).

Finally, the quality of the marriage bond derives from a combination of social self-image (individualistic, dyadic personality), sexual roles (what is required of males and females solely on the basis of their sex), the conjugal family system (the norms that prescribe and ascribe obligations and rights to family members in terms of birth order, sex, age), and the kinship system in general (the rights and obligations of related conjugal families). If this all sounds a bit complicated, that is because it really is. As a matter of fact the kinship system in the United States still eludes complete systematic analysis. What this means is that even though one might think that the kinship relationships which Americans learn from childhood and which have become integral to their personality and language are completely natural because they are taken for granted, yet they might not be that simple. First of all, kinship systems prove to be quite complicated when subject to analysis. And secondly, even the United States middle class system, the one I grew up in, is simply not all that common in the world's cultures. It is highly unlikely that a "father" in first-century Palestine—a comparison Jesus used to talk of God, our Father, the one who is in the heavens—would be the same as the "father" of Freud's central Europe or of contemporary American society.

Main Structural Features of the Kinship System Compared

Since kinship is so complicated, perhaps the easiest way to grasp the differences between our kinship norms and those of first-century Palestinian (and often Mediterranean) society is to run through our norms while contrasting them with those of our group of foreigners. We are still at a high level of abstraction, and this means that at the concrete level, not all the features listed will be perfectly and completely realized. Norms are ideal "oughts" which often get watered down in the living, yet they continually support living and serve to gauge success or failure, compliance or non-compliance. If you wonder why you should go through all this sort of "dumb" analysis, you might look at the goal of this inquiry: How can we be fair to the group of foreigners we hear when we read the New Testament? What did they mean and feel about being father, mother, husband, wife, brother, sister? What did marriage mean to them? What did divorce entail, and what was Jesus driving at when he prohibited divorce? None of these sorts of questions can be answered adequately without knowledge of kinship norms that are much like the hidden mass of an iceberg supporting the tiny, visible tip that comes through in the foregoing questions. Perhaps patience in plowing through kinship norms will yield a rewarding response to these dimensions of the New Testament.

As any Bible reader knows, the Bible is replete with kinship norms, some explicit, but most implicit. These norms change over time, from the period of Abraham the nomad, through the conquest of the land of Israel, to the post-exilic period and the time of Jesus. In what follows, I shall present the features of the American kinship system followed by corresponding features of post-exilic Judaism. We can consider pre-exilic biblical kinship features afterwards.

1) Prohibited intermarriage has as its function to prevent potentially disruptive conflicts within the kinship group. Such prohibited intermarriage is normally referred to as the incest taboo. In the United States, our norms prohibit sexual relations, hence marriage, with father, mother, child, grandparent, uncle, aunt, niece, or nephew, with twenty-nine states prohibiting first-cousin intermarriage. These are said to be "blood" relatives—a highly symbolic term.

In New Testament times, it seems the list of prohibited sexual partners from Lev. 18:6–18 and 20:11–21 were in vogue. These rules originally looked to the obligations in the area of sexual behavior of the first-born head of the group in the prime of life. They are family laws to be observed by and enforced by the head of the household in a polygamous setting. By the first century, they are understood as a list of prohibited marriage partners. If you read them patiently, you will see that they include father, mother, children, grandparents, uncles, and aunts, much like our prohibitions, aside from nieces, nephews, and cousins—these were not prohibited. However, the list also includes a series of in-laws by our reckoning, beginning with stepmothers, sisters-in-law, daughters-in-law, aunts-in-law, and their corresponding male in-laws from the female's point of view. Further, a sister-in-law of a childless marriage was to be married by a surviving brother to raise an heir for the deceased brother; this is called levirate (from Latin *levir,* meaning brother-in-law) marriage. The question I might raise here is: Were such in-laws related in law or by blood? Note that for Paul, in 1 Cor. 5:1 ff., a male is forbidden to marry his stepmother upon his father's death. This would indicate that somehow she was related by blood. Further, according to Mark 6:18, a brother was not allowed to marry his divorced sister-in-law, again indicating some sort of abiding blood relationship.

2) In the United States, marriage is monogamous, with no obligatory patterns for marrying within the kinship group, outside incest limits. Rather, marriage is generally exogamous, outside the kinship group.

In first-century Judaism among the non-elite masses, marriage was generally monogamous, much as it was among Greeks and Romans. However, in the Mediterranean world, including Judaism, there was a marked preference for keeping daughters as close to the nuclear, conjugal family as the prohibitions of incest permitted. Further, cross-cousin marriages between the offspring of the father's side of the family were also preferred. This preference—it was not an ironclad rule—is called Mediterranean "endogamy."

3) Americans make no discrimination between paternal and maternal relatives for marriage purposes when they do consider marriage within the kin group.

In the Mediterranean world, the paternal line is almost always favored, as Mediterranean "endogamy" indicates.

4) In the United States, the family name descends through the male line, but there is little other emphasis upon the male line of descent. The descent system tends to be bilineal, or, more strictly, multilineal. These first four features indicate that in our system, the ancestral lines can fan out indefinitely from any given individual, with many lines of heredity that can be emphasized for any given purpose. Thus the system of intermarriage and kinship is highly dispersed.

In the first-century world, nearly the entire emphasis is on the male line of descent. Jesus' genealogies in Matt. 1:2–16 and Luke 3:23–38 indicate this. The descent system is patrilineal, with ancestral lines focused on the father and his lineage. Thus the system of intermarriage and kinship is highly concentrated.

5) The American system emphasizes the immediate conjugal family, to the exclusion of in-laws, who are to be accorded equal treatment by the family of procreation. The conjugal family (our nuclear family) is a small, compact group of two generations (parents and their children) bound together by ties of diffuse loyalty and functioning to care for the young until they reach maturity and can repeat for themselves the process of family rearing. The age marking the end of the maturing period, the period of adolescence, now runs to about thirty; at this time persons ought be settled down and married. In this system, there are no intricate economic, political, or religious ties based on kinship, no ancestor worship, and no formal connection with remoter kin.

In the first-century Mediterranean world, the tightest unit of diffuse loyalty is the descent group of brothers and sisters whose spouses enter the kin group as strangers and remain always somewhat so. The affection we expect as a mark of the husband and wife relationship is normally a mark of brother-sister and mother-son relationships. The kin group frequently shares economic, political, and religious ties, with an awareness of and formal connection with remoter kin. This last point is illustrated by attitudes like "We have Abraham as our father" (Luke 3:8); the genealogies; and Paul's awareness of his being "of the people of Israel, of the tribe of Benjamin, a Hebrew born of Hebrews; as to the law a Pharisee" (Phil. 3:5). In this system, close relatives could legally conceal each others' offenses from the outside and worked to protect family honor (thus Jesus' family comes to remove him from an embarrassing situation in Mark 3:20–31).

6) The immediate family of father, mother, and children is usually the effective American social, residence, and consumption unit. By social consensus, the independent and autonomous conjugal unit is regarded as desirable, right, and proper. If other relatives have to live in the household, it is considered unfortunate. American parents are not to interfere with the families of their children except in extraordinary crises.

In the Mediterranean world, the household might include father, mother, the first-born son and his family, along with other unmarried children. These would live in close proximity, perhaps even sharing the same courtyard with other married sons and their families. This sort of family tends to be the effective social, residence, consumption, and production unit. Each conjugal family should be autonomous, yet the honor of the broader kin group is a concern of all, and all readily interact. This is desirable, right, and proper by social consensus. Parents readily interfere in the families of their children, and relatives in the household, especially parents, are positively regarded (along with subjects like slaves, hired laborers, and the like). Note that Simon Peter's mother-in-law lives in his house, a house in which both Simon and Andrew reside (presumably with their families, see Mark 1:29–31; Matt. 8:14–17; Luke 4:38-41; 1 Cor. 9:5, regarding Peter's wife). Further, the movement begun by Jesus is headed by "James, the Lord's brother" in Jerusalem (Gal. 1:19; see also Acts 12:17; 15:13) after the Ascension. Jesus' relatives likewise take part in the mission with their wives (1 Cor. 9:5). Note that Matthew, Mark, and Luke have no mention of Mary, the mother of Jesus, at the crucifixion scene; however, after the Resurrection, Mary and Jesus' brothers are in Jerusalem (Acts 1:14), undoubtedly having come to claim his body, as family members should.

7) In the United States, the conjugal family group is typically a consuming rather than a producing unit, especially in urban centers where the majority now live.

The preindustrial Mediterranean world is marked by families which are producing units. However, men's and women's work is sharply segregated (for example, note that the parable on anxiety in Matt. 6:25-31 has birds compared with men's work, while the lilies of the field are compared with women's work). As producing unit, the family was the focus of the activities of each family member, and potentially disruptive extrafamilial associations were taken care of by the head of the family. Similarly, membership in the craftsmen's guilds of the preindustrial city was normally based on kinship, just as membership in the elite classes derived from birth. A typical example of the family as producing unit at work is the scene of Zebedee, his sons James and John, along with hired hands in Mark 1:19–20.

8) Because the nuclear, conjugal family is the unit, and the kinship system is multilineal, American society places relatively little emphasis on family tradition and continuity. The fact that examples of "old society" (e.g., Boston, Charleston) are considered odd and humorous, along with the fact that the search for "roots" is a popular effort, only indicate that these aspects are not integral and solid parts of actual family life. At most, Americans accept limited continuity, as, for example, in name-giving.

First-century Judaism, of course, put great stress on family tradition and continuity, the traditions of Israel. From post-exilic times (read Ezra and Nehemiah) at least, genealogies, pure blood or "holy seed," and the central symbolic importance of the twelve tribes is basic. Furthermore, highly important social roles like the priesthood, requirements for admittance to the Temple, and proper marriage depended upon genealogical purity. Hence emphasis on tradition and continuity was of great concern. The Passover celebration itself understood this central concern. We shall return to it in detail later.

9) Americans enjoy a comparatively free choice of mates: free enterprise, the open market, and free competition are applied to marriage selection. This is possible because of the autonomy of the marriage unit; the married couple does not have to fit into an established broader kinship group. This is American individualism applied to marriage selection. Kin have no right to interfere, and the choice is purely individualistic. Such behavior is further bolstered by American geographical and occupational mobility, de-emphasis of kinship, and the general discontinuity of generations.

In the first-century world, we find dyadic personalities and females always embedded in some male. The choice of mates is highly limited, normally arranged by parents because the marriage pair have to fit into an established kinship group with important and complex repercussions on many other individuals. The new couple will reside within or very near one or both of the in-law families. They will maintain intimate associations with a continuous and extended kinship group. From this perspective, marriage is both a sort of treaty between groups and a personal contract between dyadic personalities. Further, these newly married dyadic personalities are in a complex and delicate state of mutual interdependence which tends to limit personal emotional feeling greatly—or at least its direct expression in action. Any considerable range of spontaneous affection would greatly impinge on the rights and obligations and interests of too many others, causing disequilibrium in the system as a whole. This need to limit spontaneous affection (e.g., to mother and son, brothers and sisters) is a basic reason why arranged marriages are usually found in kinship systems where the newly married couple is incorporated into a larger kin group.

10) In the United States, the system of residence is neo-local, that is, the newly married couple, even before the birth of their first child, resides independently of either family of orientation. They thus live independently of the restraints that might come from living in the same house as, or immediate vicinity of, their kin group.

The first-century world favored a patrilocal rule of residence. This means that the new wife would normally move in with her husband's family until such time as they could have their own residence, which in turn would be near his father's house. In this way, again, the new nuclear family has to be incorporated into the solidary, father-centered kin group. Once more, since the wider kin group preponderates, marriage tends to be an arranged union serving group interests and the needs of dyadic personality. An indication of this feature is found in Jesus' saying in Matt. 10:35: "For I have come to set a man against his father, a daughter against her mother, and a daughter-in-law against her mother-in-law" (see Luke 12:53). Note that there is no mention of son-in-law, since it was the new wife who moved into her husband's house, not the husband into the wife's family. The daughter mentioned in the saying would probably be the unmarried daughter, since she is still around to conflict with her mother.

11) American social arrangements are marked by high geograhic and social mobility. This sort of mobility results in open rather than closed social networks, with a resulting reduction of support and constraint upon marriage partners. Such arrangements bolster American individualism and affect mate choice, sex-role segregation, child-rearing, and many other aspects of family structure and process.

The first-century Mediterranean world was marked by geographical and social immobility which resulted in the heightened support and constraint of a closed social network. Such an arrangement bolsters the perception of limited good and dyadic personality. It further affects the total character of the kinship system. When each party comes to their marriage with a close-knit circle of friends and relatives who have long lived in association with them and who realistically expect to do so in the future, the marriage has to fit into social networks already firmly established. Previous relations of kinship and friendship involve strong emotional ties, reciprocal relations of support and exchange, and interlocking agreements and expectations relative to social norms and their outcomes. The obvious path of least resistance and least disruption is for the new marriage to be negotiated, and for husband and wife to maintain the segregated, although perhaps somewhat overlapping, circles of associates that they had before marriage. Bonds of affection, then, normally reside in previous settings; thus the new wife would feel close to her brothers and sisters, with her mother mourning her loss to another household, while the new husband would feel close to his brothers and sisters, maintaining close affection for his mother in whose house the new pair will take up residence. The father in each case remains an authority figure mainly concerned with his family's honor and proper maintenance.

12) The United States shows a marked tendency for adult children to disperse from the parental household even before marriage, which takes place at a rather late age. This dispersion has reached extraordinary breadth, directly tied to vertical mobility between classes. Children need not remain in the class of their parents, and often do not.

In the first-century world, adult male children normally stay within or close by the parental household, while females are married out. Usually the first-born male will inherit his father's house; hence he remains in the household, with his married brothers living nearby. Males follow the occupation of their father and remain in the same inherited social class. In the parental household, the father is primarily responsible for those aspects of life that relate the family to the larger social environment.

13) Finally, in the United States there is an effective norm against discussing marital or family problems with relatives or friends—a result of the social isolation of the nuclear family. Instead of family and friends, such problems are normally brought to experts like the clergy, marriage counselors, physicians, and the like.

In the first-century world, marital problems were discussed with brothers and sisters, not with parents or friends. In the book of Ecclesiasticus, there is a suggestive list of things to be ashamed of and not ashamed of (41:17—42:8), and the list is headed with this advice: "Be ashamed of immorality [literally: lewdness, sexual matters] before your father or mother." But given the foregoing features of the first-century Mediterranean kinship system, the expectations engendered in the dyadic personalities involved would not generate our sorts of marital problems. For social life is so organized that men and women move at ease in two exclusive circles that might touch but never overlap, even on domestic occasions. These circles coincide with the sexual and moral division of labor mentioned in chapter 2 on honor and shame.

Marriage

In the first-century Mediterranean world and earlier, marriage symbols the fusion of the honor of two extended families and is undertaken with a

view to political and/or economic concerns—even when it might be
defensively confined to coreligionist, as in first-century Judaism. As a
process, marriage is the disembedding of the prospective wife from her
family by means of a ritual positive challenge (i.e., gifts and/or services to
her father) by the father of the prospective groom, along with her father's
response. Should the father be unavailable, then responsible male members
of the family, like older brothers, uncles, or the prospective groom himself,
take part in the transaction. During this initial phase, the prospective
spouses are set apart for each other; they are betrothed, "hallowed," or
"sanctified" (which is what "set apart" means in Hebrew/Aramaic). The
responsible males draw up a marriage contract, and eventually the bride's
father must surrender his daughter to the groom, who takes a wife by
bringing her into his house. The parable of the ten maidens in Matt. 25:1–12
pictures the bridegroom coming home, obviously with his bride (not
mentioned in the R.S.V., but in some ancient texts). With the ritual movement
of the bride into the bridegroom's house, the marriage process is complete.
The wife-taking always results in the embedding of the female in the honor
of her husband. She, in turn, symbols the shame of the new family—its
sensitivity to public opinion and for its own self-image.

These stages of the marriage process seem to be alluded to by Paul in 1
Cor. 7:29–31 in somewhat of a reverse order: "let those who have wives live
as though they had none [= the married couple], and those who mourn as
though they were not mourning [= bride's family losing their
daughter/sister], and those who rejoice as though they were not rejoicing
[= groom's family and their gain], and those who buy as though they had no
goods [= groom's family who must pay bridewealth at betrothal], and those
who deal with the world as though they had no dealings with it"
[= bride's family dealing at betrothal for suitable bridewealth; I follow J.
Duncan M. Derrett in this explanation].

The bride's family looks for a groom who will be a good provider, a kind
father, and a respected citizen. The bride does not look to him for
companionship or comfort. Instead, as in all societies that exalt bonds
between males and masculine lines of rights, the new wife will not be
integrated into her husband's family, but will remain for the most part of her
life on the periphery of the husband's family. As a rule, she is like a
"stranger" in the house, a sort of long-lost relative of unknown quality. Just
as life in the Mediterranean world is so organized that men and women move
in exclusive circles that might touch but never overlap, so marriage is simply
one phase of contact between male and female circles, with no overlapping
expected. When does the wife shed the stranger's role? First of all, when she
is the mother of a son: the birth of a son assures her security and status
recognition in her husband's family. The son grows up to be his mother's ally

and advocate of her interests, not only against his father, but against his own wife. In case of conflict in the household, daughters-in-law do not stand a chance. Thus the wife's most important relationship in the family is that to her son. Daughters are welcome but burdensome, since they can plague a father's honor. Sirach notes: "A daughter keeps her father secretly wakeful, and worry over her robs him of sleep; when she is young, lest she do not marry, or if married, lest she be hated; while a virgin, lest she be defiled or become pregnant in her father's house; or having a husband, lest she prove unfaithful, or though married, lest she be barren. Keep strict watch over a headstrong daughter, lest she make you a laughing stock to your enemies, a byword in the city and notorious among the people and put you to shame before the great multitude" (Ecclesiasticus 42:9–11).

Further, a female is not a stranger when she is a sister, especially with brothers. Brother and sister share the most intense cross-sexual relationship in this sort of cultural arrangement, so much so that the brother readily gets highly incensed when an unauthorized male approaches either his wife or his sister. Should a woman misbehave sexually, the father will hold his daughter responsible, while the brother will seek out the other party and attempt revenge. The last point is illustrated in the Bible most clearly in 2 Sam. 13:1–29, and somewhat in Gen. 34:1–31, although this last passage indicates that Jacob was not angered over his daughter Dinah's behavior, just her brothers'. We shall consider these passages shortly. Here we will only note that the husband-wife relationship does not supercede the intense relationship between brother and sister. Thus, should the brother reside near his sister, and his sister and her husband quarrel and separate, this would be a matter of little more than inconvenience and mild regret to her and her brothers and sisters. Consequently, stability of marriage would be highest when the wife is decisively separated from her kin group of origin and is socially incorporated (by means of a son) into the kin group of her husband.

Finally, the new wife would not be a stranger if she married a parallel cousin, a sort of surrogate brother. This is as close as she might marry in her kin group, given first-century incest taboos, although some males did marry nieces, as complaints from Qumran indicate. However, these last two categories would not be that prevalent, and the normal situation of new wives would be like that of strangers in their husbands' houses.

Given the foregoing definition of marriage, divorce would be the reversal of the process described above. Hence divorce means the process of disembedding the female from the honor of the male, along with a sort of redistribution and return of the honor of the families concerned. Now the extent to which the wife becomes embedded in her husband upon marriage as well as the extent of the disembedding effected by divorce would depend upon the type of marriage strategies and marriage norms involved. In the Bible there are three major sets of marriage strategies, and to gain a better understanding of what the New Testament says about marriage and divorce, it might serve us well to consider the Old Testament background to the New Testament discussion.

Marriage Strategies in the Bible

From beginning to end, the books of the Bible reveal people much concerned with honor and shame, interacting in an agonistic way. Marriage, too, is part of the agonistic give and take of challenge and response which we have previously considered. With this sort of social setting for interaction, it would follow that like other challenge-response strategies, marriage strategies might be of three types. Thus in a challenge situation I might readily give in to you for my benefit (conciliatory); I might attempt to struggle with you for some sort of supremacy (aggressive); or I might just ignore you and stick to my group entirely (defensive). Each strategy would entail a range of styles or permissible expressions, yet the focus would be either conciliation, aggression, or defense. When it comes to marriage strategies, it does in fact seem that the broad periods of the history of Israel were characterized by distinctive strategies, with conciliation typical of the patriarchal period, aggression typical of the Israelite, pre-exilic period, and defense typical of the post-exilic, Jewish period. Mediterranean "endogamy," the preference for keeping daughters close to the nuclear family, seems constantly to have been the ideal. Let us briefly consider the evidence.

The Patriarchal Period. While we obviously lack a wide range of data for this period, it is not too difficult to see that the seminomadic patriarchs enshrined the endogamous ideal. Abraham married his half-sister (Gen. 20:12), Nahor married his brother's daughter, his niece (Gen. 11:29); Isaac married his father's brother's son's daughter, his first cousin's daughter (Gen. 24:15); Esau, among others, married his father's brother's daughter, his paternal parallel cousin (Gen. 29:10); Jacob married his mother's brother's daughters, his maternal parallel cousins (Gen. 29:10); Amram, Moses's father, married his father's sister, his paternal aunt (Exod. 6:20; Num. 26:57–59).

From the traditions recorded in the Bible, we find that these seminomads took a marriage strategy that was *conciliatory*—and by marriage strategy I specifically mean behavior based on the perception of how the female is embedded in the male's honor. The patriarchs readily give their women in exchange for political protection and/or economic advantage after marriage, although preferring to retain them for themselves in marriage if possible. They are willing to offer their wives and married daughters to higher class, usually sedentary urbanites for political and economic ends. This was the strategy of Abraham with Pharaoh (Gen. 12:10–20); of Lot with his daughters, even in the presence of their husbands (Gen. 19:12–16, 31–38); of Abraham and Abimelech (Gen. 20:2–18, and note especially v. 13 for Abraham's habitual seminomadic attitude: "And when God caused me to wander from my father's house, I said to her, 'This is the kindness you must do me: at every place to which we come, say of me, He is my brother.' "); of Jacob with his daughter Dinah (Gen. 34:1 ff., and note Jacob's curse on Simeon and Levi for avenging their sister in Gen. 49:5–7). Thus sexual hospitality, specifically to one of higher social class and for the controlling male's benefit, was the social norm. Sacred prostitution, a form of sexual hospitality, would also be found in this period. The disembedded female, notably widows in our evidence, could readily dishonor the male by proving too aggressive (thus the daughters of Lot in Gen. 19:31–38; the daughter-in-law of Judah in Gen. 38). Incest with one's father's wife or concubine dishonors the father and hence is a grave insult symboling revolt against paternal authority (for Reuben, see Gen. 35:21–22; Gen. 49:3–4).

Typical of the period are plural wives (i.e., a legal, first-rank wife along with concubines or legal second-rank wives), marriage with widows, foreigners, slaves, and the like (see Gen. 16:1–4; 25:1–6 for Abraham; Gen. 24:67 for Isaac; Gen. 26:34; 28:9 for Esau; Gen. 29:21; 30:12 for Jacob). Inheritance is patrilineal, and residence after marriage is normally patrilocal.

We might characterize the patriarchal period as symboled by the family, a sacred or holy family chosen by God and consisting of the patriarch and his offspring. The patriarch heads this family, with worship centered in the family and with norms governing social interaction deriving from family custom.

The Israelite Period. The story of Shechem (Gen. 34) foreshadows a new set of kinship norms that characterize the marriage strategy of the Israelite period and that are codified in the early laws of Israel. In the story, Simeon and Levi, unlike their father Jacob, display an *aggressive* marriage strategy: they would deny their women to higher class outsiders and even attempt to take the outsiders' women. In other words, their wives and sisters are perceived as embedded in their honor to such an extent that they feel compelled to defend that honor even in face of higher class encroachment. Sexual hospitality is a thing of the past.

With this sort of behavior and its expression in subsequent law codes, the purity or shame of women becomes attached to male honor in such a way that it cannot be even temporarily disembedded. Once this happens, marriage strategy loses the potential for reciprocity that it has in the conciliatory mode. Now marriage strategy emerges exclusively as an agonistic value, a competition in which the winners are those who keep their daughters, sisters, and wives and take the women of other groups in addition, giving only their patronage, their power, and their protection in exchange.

In the new ideology, males are now clearly vulnerable to varying degrees through their wives, daughters, and sisters. Aggressive strategy demands that fathers attempt to choose as mates for their daughters those who are closest and best known and who somehow already share in the collective honor of the patriline. The fathers of the patriarchal period, on the other hand, are more concerned about their sons than their daughters. In the aggressive perspective, daughters should marry relatives as close to home as incest rules allow. Sons, on the other hand, should marry non-relatives, but bring the spouse into the patrilocal community. In this way the honorable aggressive head of the house gains sons-in-law, retains sons and daughters, and gains daughters-in-law along with a range of offspring. Given this sort of preference, marriage ends up being a competitive, agonistic affair of power in which there are winners and losers of women, more powerful and less powerful patrons and clients, and social classes between which a certain mobility of family statuses takes place. This is simply an expression of the agonistic quality of social relations typical of sedentary Mediterranean communities from antiquity.

For the winners the result of such strategy is an increase in numbers, hence political power, along with the ability to acquire more women in exchange for patronage while avoiding the risks to honor by giving one's daughter away. Thus the competition for women in marriage negotiations is a competition for power. Provided that sons born of such unions can be kept faithful to the patriline, those heads of families with the most women expand fastest and attain a position of domination. This, of course, presupposes polygamy, with the corresponding problem of how much trust a father can have in his foreign wives and their sons.

Consider the biblical texts from the pre-exilic period. The importance of many wives in the struggle for power is noted for Gideon (Judges 8:30), and subsequently for the kings of Israel, notably David (1 Sam. 25:39–43; 27:3; 2 Sam. 3:2–5), and notoriously Solomon (I Kings 11:1 ff.). The problem of the degree of trust one can have in foreign wives and their sons is signaled in the story of Abimelech's return to his matriline (Judges 9) as well as in the various stratagems of the king's sons, beginning with Absalom (2 Sam. 13:30). Numerous foreign wives mean trouble, or so the authors of the book of Kings think (of Solomon, 1 Kings 11:1–3; of Rehoboam, 1 Kings 14:21–24; of Asa, 1 Kings 15:11–14; 22:46).

The ideology of conquest and consolidation in the Israelite period envisions a land in which the Israelites will gain wives and daughters but give away no sons (e.g., Exod. 34:14–16, later tempered by Deut. 7:1–6; Joshua

23:11–13). The legislation of the period, both the early material in Exodus and Numbers and the later formulation in Deuteronomy, looks to solidifying as well as controlling those aspects of the aggressive strategy that might disturb the public order sanctioned by God and the king. Sexual hospitality, both public and private (i.e., the prostitution of one's daughter, sister, or wife), is now perceived as an affront against the male in whom the female is embedded (Deut. 23:17–18). The married female is now so fully embedded in the male that any dealing with the wife is invariably perceived as an affront to male honor; it now becomes inconceivable for an honorable male to offer his wife in hospitality to another (Exod. 20:14, 17; Deut. 5:18, 21; 2 Sam. 3:6–11). Adultery, of course, symbols grave trespass into the space of a fellow honorable male, a clear negative challenge requiring vengeance as a response.

The limits of incest are spelled out (Deut. 22:30 [in Hebrew texts 23:1]; 27:20–23; yet in 1 Chron. 2:24, Caleb is said to marry his step-mother), and incest still serves as an outraging symbol of revolt against one's patron-father (2 Sam. 16:20–22: Absalom and David's concubines; 1 Kings 2:13–17: Adonijah and Solomon's concubine). Concubines might be available from war (Deut. 21:10–17; see Num. 31:18) and through debt-bondage from one's fellow Israelite (Exod. 21:7–11). However, eloping with an unmarried and unbetrothed girl—the passage is often interpreted as rape and seduction—does not make the girl one's own, but rather the girl's father alone has the right to determine the girl's future (Exod. 22:16–17; Deut. 22:23–27). The father has the right because sexual dealings with his daughters are an affront to his honor and would lead her brothers to avenge her.

Since marriage transactions entail the mutual honor of the families concerned, such dealings are to be carried out fairly and without deception to prevent vengeance and feuding. The regulation on the tokens of virginity in Deut. 22:13–21 point to this. However, the tokens of virginity—the female's blood from the ruptured maidenhead shed on first intercourse—have somewhat deeper symbolic implications. Just as the maidenhead symbols shame, so in the process of first intercourse the first wife of a male's youth becomes the bearer of the male's and the subsequent family's shame—their sensitivity to honor. Further, the blood on both conjugal partners symbols that their marriage is a type of blood relationship—the husband "cleaves to his wife, and they become one flesh" (Gen. 2:24). Thus the emphasis on blood in the marriage process indicates that marriage is not simply a sort of legal contract, but essentially a blood relationship in which the stranger wife becomes a member of the husband's patriline. This blood relationship subsequently entails certain contractual obligations between the families and the marriage partners as well. In the aggressive strategy, the husband retains the right to disembed his wife from his honor should she dishonor him. This is the right to divorce in Deut. 24:1. This right to divorce in the deuteronomic legislation is probably a compromise solution in favor of peace between families and public order. The reason I say this is that in situations that dishonor the male and involve blood relatives, the normal solution is to kill the one who causes dishonor (thus the wicked son in Deut. 21:18–21; the wicked daughter in Deut. 22:20–21). In the case of the duly married dishonoring wife, divorce is the available compromise solution. The certificate of divorce of Deut. 24:1 indicates that the previous male cedes his rights over the female, hence that he will not be dishonored if the female marries again. However, he cannot take her back after a subsequent marriage because such behavior is tantamount to sexual hospitality. Sexual hospitality is prohibited in the aggressive strategy; any return to conciliatory strategy is "an abomination before the Lord" (Deut. 24:4). Finally, to prevent embedded females from dishonoring the male by entering into formal contractual obligations, the male has the right to rescind them (Num. 30:2 ff.). Only males have the prerogative of entering formal contractual arrangements, yet widows and unmarried divorcees—unembedded, previously married females—can act as males in this regard, hence their ambiguous social status. The parameters for vengeance that might arise from aggressive strategies are also spelled out (Num. 35:16–28).

The laws of Israel from this period come from the political institution symboled by the palace-temple (in Hebrew, the same word stands for both palace and temple, normally built adjacent to each other). The political institution would seek to impose its laws by force, while custom would work to contravene the law. That customs from the conciliatory phase were still present is evidenced by the complaints of the prophets against sacred prostitution, e.g., Hos. 4:14–19; Jer. 5:7–9; 7:16 ff. (the queen of heaven in this last text is probably the virgin to whom Job [31:1] does not lift his eyes). For a fuller picture, see the exilic reminiscences of Ezekiel 16:22.

We might characterize the Israelite period as symboled in the Holy Land, the land set apart by God for his people, a land ultimately under his control. Authority over this land lies in the hands of a leader/king. Worship is disengaged from the family and situated first in various local shrines, then in a centralized shrine under the control of priestly families. The norms found in the customs of the elite become codified in law—the law of Moses, which is the law of God.

The Jewish Period. Judaism gets its name from the land of Judea, and the beginnings of Judaism are rooted in the Judean exiles and their return to their pre-exilic homeland. The experience of the exile and the return mark a change in the central symbols of Israel, hence in marriage strategy as well. The accounts of the return in the books of Ezra and Nehemiah indicate that not a few of the returning exiles, in order to fit into the prevailing society of Judea as they found it, divorced their wives and married into local families. Such behavior on the part of both the families occupying the land and the returnees was a mutual conciliatory gesture. The book of Malachi sets the tone for this period in the area of marriage strategy, with its insistance that what God desires is "godly offspring." "For I hate divorce, says the LORD the God of Israel, and covering one's garment with violence" (Mal. 2:13–16). In the circumstances addressed by Malachi, what God hates is the divorce of Jew and Jew; there is silence about the divorce of Jew and non-Jew. Be that as it may, the reforms of Ezra and Nehemiah require the divorce of all wives (and their children) acquired by the returning exiles from native families, along with marriage to fellow Jews only. Thus, due to the priestly reform of post-exilic Yahwism and its demand for fidelity to the covenant, the marriage strategy worked out in Ezra-Nehemiah leads to a *defensive* strategy: females born within the covenant are to be kept, and entanglement with foreign women is to be resolutely avoided (read Neh. 9—10 and Ezra 9—10).

This defensive strategy would lead the newly formed, closed Jewish community to monogamy (unlike the aggressive posture adopted in Islam). Further, the prohibition of divorce as proclaimed by Malachi is antipolygamy in its effects, whether polygamy be successive or simultaneous. It is this defensive marriage strategy coupled with the perception that embeds female sexual purity in male honor that lies at the bottom of the sexual behavior found in the Priestly writings of the Old Testament. These gradually are developed by "tradition" into the norms of first-century Palestine. The laws from the previous strategy, as well as the customs of the patriarchal stories, have to be reshaped to fit the new strategy. The earlier creation story of Gen. 2:4 ff. is prefaced by a priestly creation story in which God's first command to man is to increase and multiply (Gen. 1:28), which is, of course, in line with the defensive marriage strategy set out in the rest of the priestly writings.

The holiness code of the priestly tradition is a purity code (see next chapter), a set of explicitly formulated social lines that are to clearly mark "us" (Jews) off from "them" (non-Jews). This set of boundaries is replicated in temple structure, in sacrifice procedures, and, for our purposes, in sexual behavior. The general principle is that everything is forbidden unless it fits within its designated social space. Legislation specifies designated social spaces. To begin with, early Israelite customs on forbidden sexual relations are restated as incest lines of prohibited degrees of marriage in Lev. 18:6–18; 20:11–12, 14, 20. Adultery is not only an outrage to male honor, but also an abomination (Lev. 18:20; 20:10). Sexual hospitality (Lev. 19:29), keeping

Israelite women as slave-wives (Lev. 25:44–46), homosexuality (Lev. 18:22; 20:13), priestly marriages with once-embedded or shamed women (Lev. 21:7, 13–14; see Ezek. 44:22)—all these are not simply affronts to male honor, but equally abominations before the Lord. Male honor is symboled in the male sexual organs, and both the priest (Lev. 21:20) and the non-priest (as in the previous period, Deut. 23:1) must have their sexual organs intact to be full members of the community.

Since holy seed or holy offspring are paramount symbols, genealogies tracing holy seed come to have emphatic symbolic importance (read the genealogies in Ezra and Nehemiah; also in the books of Judith and Tobit). Sexual bodily effluvia render a person unclean (Lev. 15:16–18, 32 for the layman; Lev. 22:4 for the priest; Lev. 15:19–30 for the female; the new defensiveness is clearly articulated in the rules about sexual relations during menstruation in Lev. 15:24; 18:19; 20:18). Homosexuality dishonors the male (one partner plays a female role) and confuses defensive boundaries—and it is an abomination to the Lord (Lev. 18:22; 20:13). Bestiality applies to males as well as females (Lev. 18:23; 20:15–16). Finally, while sexual hospitality or sacred prostitution is dishonoring and forbidden (Lev. 19:29), sexual intercourse with a slave woman is frowned upon as defiling (Lev. 19:20) and requires a guilt offering. So much for the law.

In the customs of the period, the sages warn against adultery because of the vengeance that will surely come from the outraged husband (Prov. 6:25–35). The woman most likely to be unfaithful are those whose husbands do not stay at home: "For my husband is not at home; he has gone on a long journey; he took a bag of money with him; at full moon he will come home" (Prov. 7:19–20; see 9:13–18). This text implies, again, that the trader not only offends against the common sense of limited good, but has not enough honor to keep his wife properly cordoned off.

Perhaps the most information about the customs of defensive strategy is to be found in Ecclesiasticus, the book of Sirach, who wrote about 150 B.C. in Jerusalem. This is urban elite information, the sort of ideal norms toward which the non-elites aspire. To begin with, Sirach tells us that fathers arrange marriages (7:25; see 2 Esdras 9:47 for a mother who arranges the marriage, perhaps in default of a father). In the Hebrew and Syriac text of Ecclesiasticus 7:23, the father is told: "Do you have sons? Correct them, and choose wives for them while they are young." This points to the practice of early arranged marriages in which the father engages the girl for his son and vice versa before either of them are of marriage age, puberty. Children owe their lives to their parents, a debt which they can never adequately repay (7:28). In his advice to married men in 9:1–9, Sirach offers counsel on attitudes toward various classes of women. The married man ought to avoid unmarried women because of penalties that might be exacted—presumably by her brothers and father (9:5); and married women ensnare a man in the vengeance of their husbands (9:8–9). Prostitutes lead to a loss of inheritance, either because any offspring remain "fatherless," or because the man's father would be shamed by his sons' actions (9:6).

Sirach views the wife as embedded in her husband, since divorce means to "cut her off from your flesh" (25:26); this is further indication that marriage is considered a sort of blood relationship, resulting in "one flesh," much as children are "one flesh" with their parents. Daughters marry out; they live in their husbands' families although even there a daughter can still shame her father (22:3–6, note v. 3: "the birth of a daughter is a loss"). Ecclesiasticus 25:16—26:27 discusses the range of wifely behavior, from shameful to honorable, including rival wives. An important cultural value is alluded to by Sirach in Ecclesiasticus 25:21, where the ideal wife is one who is beautiful and wealthy (note that Judith is such an ideal female, yet a widow who does not remarry: Judith 8:1–8; also Sarah, the future wife of Tobit, is such: Tobit 6:11–12). However, by means of marriage, the wealth of the female should pass to the male, for "there is wrath and impudence and great disgrace when a wife supports her husband" (Ecclesiasticus 25:22). The story of the younger Tobit indicates his proper social placement, since Sarah belongs to his patriline and her wealth belongs to him should he marry her (Tobit 6:11).

As mentioned above, the father is all too vulnerable through his daughters (Ecclesiasticus 26:10–12 and especially 42:9–11). Hence the cultural imperative to marry them off as soon as possible, which means shortly after the onset of menstruation. Because they are embedded in the male, women can all too easily shame their fathers and husbands. Thus, "better is the wickedness of a man than a woman who does good; and it is a woman who brings shame and disgrace" (Ecclesiasticus 42:14; note 40:19: Even in defensive strategy, where offspring are all important, a blameless wife is better than children and the honor that comes from giving public endowments).

This defensive marriage strategy stands as the basic perspective and chief mode of perception for the discussions of marital and sexual behavior in the Qumran writings, the writings of the early rabbis, as well as the reactions of Jesus recorded rather differently in Matthew, Mark, and Luke. In the non-legal texts of the period, like Ecclesiasticus, Tobit, and Judith, a person's intentions, his heart, counts in sexual encounters. The focus of this intention in marriage is on offspring, on holy seed, this being the sole valid motivating factor in sexual encounters. Any lesser motives are shameful. Thus Tobit's wedding night sexual union with Sarah is motivated not by her wealth and beauty, but by holy seed (the former being called immorality or immoral motives, the later truth—Tobit 8:7). Likewise, in early rabbinic Judaism, marriage entered into because of the beauty or wealth of the bride is equivalent to immorality; offspring of such marriages are almost tantamount to bastards, the symbolic opposite of holy seed. Thus, given this emphasis on defensive strategy and holy seed, imputations of doubtful lineage are among the gravest insults in the culture, sure to get prompt attention, for example, John the Baptist's calling the Pharisees and Sadducees of Jerusalem a "brood of vipers" (Matt. 3:7; Luke 3:7; Jesus uses the term according to Matt. 12:34; 23:33) means nothing less than "snake bastards," a doubly offensive term. Similarly, Jesus calls his contemporaries an "adulterous generation" (Mark 8:38; Matt. 12:39; 16:4), literally a generation of bastards, the offspring of adulterous unions. These are powerful insults in a culture where purity of lineage is a central concern. Jesus' parable on divorce, with remarriage called adultery, likewise implies bastard offspring in such a union (Mark 10:11; Matt. 5:32; 19:19; Luke 16:18). Jesus' teaching on divorce will be considered below, in the hypothesis-testing section of this chapter.

Now we might characterize the post-exilic, Jewish period as focused on the symbol of holy offspring. These holy offspring form a holy people, headed by priests, with worship in the central Temple in the central preindustrial city. Norms for the period derive from priestly law that covers the behavior of priest and non-priest alike.

When we turn to the New Testament and the typically Christian marriage strategies developed in early Christian communities, we find that they are in most respects continuations of the defensive strategy of Judaism. For these early communities, the Bible means the Old Testament, the Bible of Judaism. With this in mind, consider the churches of Paul and the churches after Paul as mirrored in the New Testament. I present them as prolongations of the defensive strategy, hence the name "Pauline interval."

The Pauline Interval. With Paul and the early Christian communities that nurtured him, a new twist on the defensive marriage strategy develops. It does not cover any lengthy period, but an interval between Paul and the post-Pauline churches. The basis for this strategy is Paul's conviction that all people can have equal access to God in Christ regardless of sexual roles, ethnicity, or social status (read Gal. 3:27–28; see also Rom. 10:12; 1 Cor. 12:13; Col. 3:11, which is probably a baptismal formula). Since in Paul's Jewish world, norms about sexual behavior, ethnicity, and social status all derived from the Torah, the Old Testament, and since Paul rejects the Torah as normative for Christians, he thus rejects Torah laws about sexual behavior, ethnicity, and social status for Christians. What he does is reject law and revert to custom. Let me explain this point for a moment.

For analyzing Paul, it is important to understand the difference between law and custom. Relationships between human beings are patterned and controlled by more or less obvious rules of behavior, by "oughts." Such rules of behavior or "oughts" are called norms. Now both law and custom have this in common, that they are bodies or series or collections of norms. The difference between law and custom is sanction, that is, who puts the teeth into the norms when you do not follow them, who enforces the norm. Custom is sanctioned by the same social institutions that the norms themselves create, while law is sanctioned by some other institutions, specifically some form of political institution. If this is too abstract, consider the following example. Why do you treat your parents like parents, and why do they treat you like their children? The norms and oughts of parent behavior and affection toward their children, as well as the norms and oughts of children's behavior and affection toward their parents, make up an aspect of what is called the family. The family, in this aspect of parent-child relationship, consists of such reciprocal norms of behavior. The norms create the institution. Now what if the state or national government passes a directive that says parents and children must treat each other properly and with affection. What the government is doing is taking a custom from family behavior, from the family institution, and doubly institutionalizing it by having government power enforce and sanction what was previously custom. Law is always a custom that has been doubly institutionalized— from the sphere of family, economics, religion, or education, all of which consist of norms that are customary. People follow rules in their family interactions, in their economic dealings, in their religious approaches to God and fellow men, and in their teaching each other the traditions of our society even before they find out that the government in question might take certain aspects of their behavior in these areas and make those customary norms binding on all in the group with the teeth that government can provide.

Furthermore, social institutions can become so complex that they formalize certain norms and outfit themselves with little quasi-political bodies called administrations that in turn raise what was previously custom to law. Administrations then act as a type of enforcing agency for the laws thus doubly institutionalized. So, for example, universities and colleges have administrations that make laws which consist of previous customary behavior. These laws work in the university like national laws work in the nation and are often further sanctioned by the national government; thus, they are institutionalized three times. The same holds for religious bodies. They, too, when complex enough, set up administrations that give a political cast to previous custom, thus doubly institutionalizing religious norms and making them laws.

Now when I say that Paul rejects law and reverts to custom, what I mean is that he no longer recognizes the political institution of Judaism consisting of the priestly elite of Jerusalem, the Sanhedrin, and their formalized norms, the Torah. He thus rejects the Jewish priestly system and its sanctions in favor of norms and sanctions deriving from the interacting partners within the group—in his case, the dyadic persons interacting within the community called the church. The customs Paul envisions as binding Christians in their reciprocal interactions derive from the activity of God's power, the Spirit, within those communities. This I would call a *charismatic* strategy. Recall what was said about the Spirit and dyadic personality above.

However, Paul also insists that his fellow Christians not confuse societal realities (the laws of the Greek, Roman, and Jewish world) with the open access to God and the "oughts" flowing from this access as symboled in Christ. Rather, Christian custom and societal law now stand in dialectical opposition. This means that they mutually influence each other in Paul's period of spontaneous expectation of the return of Christ. On the one hand, openness to God and neighbor is necessary and can be fully expressed in Christian gatherings, but in line with the customs thus far developed in the Christian churches (thus 1 Cor. 11:2–16; note v.16: "we recognize no other practice, nor do the churches of God"). On the other hand, the opinion of outsiders (societal reality, prevailing law) is to be taken into account. The presumption is that Christian custom is to be at least as good as the best in surrounding cultures (e.g., 1 Cor. 5:1). Hence Christians need only do what is honorable in Christ, regardless of the law. "Whatever is true, whatever is honorable, whatever is just, whatever is pure, whatever is lovely, whatever is gracious, if there is any excellence, if there is anything worthy of praise, think about these things. What you have learned and received and heard and seen in me, do; and the God of peace will be with you" (Phil. 4:8–9).

In the light of the prevailing cultural context, I would call Paul's marriage strategy a *charismatic defensive* strategy. It is charismatic insofar as it derives from Christian custom, and it is defensive insofar as the norms for sexual encounter have to at least match the best in Jewish and Greek legal tradition, which was defensive.

The prevalent symbols of the Pauline interval are holy group (the church of the saints) headed by charismatic leaders, with worship centered in the prayer and activity of the group. Their norms derive from their customs. Within the framework of these symbols, Paul is still concerned about holy seed (1 Cor. 7:13–14), a point he refers to as he deals with Jesus' parable about divorce, now taken as Christian norm (1 Cor. 7:10–11). First

Corinthians 7 deals mainly with the problem posed by the Corinthians as to whether sexual relations are allowed for Christians; the chapter is not really about marriage and the relationship of husband and wife in marriage. Paul's advice, though, is that Christians ought to stay in the marriages they had when they became Christian, but if the unbelieving partner causes difficulty, peace is a greater value than preserving the marriage (1 Cor. 7:15). But for new marriages and remarriages, these should take place "in the Lord" (1 Cor. 7:39; 2 Cor. 6:14—7:1), presumaby with fellow Christians. This feature marks a centripetal direction of social interaction within the holy group, a form of defensive strategy in which those in the group intermarry without divorce. This strategy is further developed in the subsequent period.

The Post-Pauline Period. The post-Pauline development of Christianity discernible in the New Testament marks a consolidation of the charismatic customs developed previously. Christian custom moves on the way to becoming Christian law, with sanctions deriving from the governing body (administration) of the group. Now, due to the general obligations· of Christianity and fidelity to the new covenant demanded by them, women born within the new covenant or entering the group in an unmarried state are to be kept, and marital entanglements with outsiders are to be avoided. This strategy is a defensive marriage strategy, but it now takes place in Christ, hence a form of *Christian defensive* strategy. And predictably, the new Christian norms are much like the old defensive rules of Judaism, but are now outfitted with Christian motivation. We find such rules in Eph. 5:22 ff.; Col. 3:18 ff.; 1 Peter 2:11—3:12; 1 Tim. 2:8–15; 4:1–5; 5:3–16.

This post-Pauline period is likewise the time in which the Gospels are written down. Matthew, Mark, and Luke, as previously mentioned, each present a tradition in which Jesus' parable on divorce is shaped into a type of Christian norm, further underscoring Christian defensive marriage strategy. About A.D. 106, Ignatius, bishop of Antioch, urges that marriages of Christians take place before the local bishop, a procedure that is within the same strategy.

What characterizes the post-Pauline development of Christianity is the symbol of holy church, an association of dyadic personalities who are to keep the association holy. The association is headed by duly chosen officers, with worship gradually localized. Developing custom now takes on the quality of law, administered by duly chosen officers.

The main structural features of the kinship system described at the beginning of this chapter for the Mediterranean world would apply to both the defensive strategy of Judaism and the defensive strategy of post-Pauline Christianity. For the New Testament reader, it should be useful to know that these kinship features were the ones shared both by Jesus' audience and by the early Christian churches who collected the New Testament writings.

Summary

Kinship and its major generating institution, marriage, deal with the meanings and values embodied by persons who are involved in the birth of a child and the process begun by birth. This process, from the perspective of kinship, covers the developing web-work of human relations—by blood and in law—rooted in the culturally interpreted fact of birth. Birth, of course, is the effect of the union of a male and a female human being who share some sort of previous relationship. When this relationship is one that agrees with the kinship norms of a society, it is called marriage. Kinship and marriage are sets of social norms that can be analyzed into a range of features. Distinctive features of kinship norms in first-century Palestinian society include incest taboos, monogamy, a sort of endogamy, emphasis on the male line of descent, patrilocal marriage, a somewhat extended family living arrangement, the family as unit of production, emphasis on family traditions, arranged marriages, geographic and social immobility, ties of affection between brothers and sisters and mothers and children rather than between husband and wife, and the wife as a blood relation who often remained a stranger in the house.

In the first-century Mediterranean world, marriage means the fusion of the honor of two extended families, undertaken with a view to political and/or economic considerations. Marriage is a process of disembedding the female from her family and embedding her in her husband—and his family. Females are always perceived as embedded in some male unless they find themselves in the anomalous situation of being a widow or divorcee without kin.

The first-century Jews followed a marriage strategy that might be called defensive, while the Bible evidences two other forms of strategy as well, the conciliatory and the aggressive. The patriarchal period reveals a conciliatory marriage strategy marked by endogamy and sexual hospitality toward persons of higher social rank, with a view to the economic and political benefit of the male. The Israelite period is marked by an aggressive marriage strategy in which power comes from the possesion of females and their offspring, with a resulting emphasis on polygamy, wife-taking from other groups, and the refusal of daughers to outsiders if possible. The Jewish period, the period of the ministry of John the Baptist and Jesus, is characterized by a defensive strategy in which the marriage partners should both be under the covenant, with the avoidance of foreigners altogether. During the interval of expectation of the return of the Lord evidenced in Paul's writings, the defensive strategy of Judaism is maintained but interpreted in the light of developing Christian custom. In the post-Pauline writings, these developing Christian customs become law for the Christian movement, and a Christian defensive marriage strategy gets under way. The main features of each of these periods are set out in Figure 4.

Figure 4: *Marriage Strategies in the Bible*

Marriage and Kinship	Conciliatory	Aggressive	Defensive	Charismatic Defensive	Christian Defensive
Main Symbol:	Holy Family	Holy Land	Holy Seed	Holy Churches	Holy Church
Period:	Patriarchal	Israelite	Jewish	Pauline	Post-Pauline
Head:	Patriarch	Leader/King	Priest	Charismatic Leaders	Church Officers (Bishop)
Norms:	Custom	Law	Law	Custom	Law
Worship:	Family	Temple/ Palace	Temple Group Activity	Group Activity	Church Group Activity

From the Pauline perspective (read Galatians 3—4), we can further describe these periods as:

Promise	Law	Law	Fulfilled Promise	New Law
Abrahamic Covenant	Sinai Covenant	Ezra Covenant	New Covenant	New Covenant

Old Jerusalem   **New Jerusalem**
in Israel   **in Christ**

Testing the Hypothesis

The models presented in this chapter include a set of features of the kinship system and a set of marriage strategies. Throughout the chapter I have made reference to a large number of biblical passages which are not cited in the text. Consequently, the first step toward validating or invalidating the models presented here is for you to read all the texts cited above. As you read the texts, judge whether they fit the model or not. Can you think of some other model in which the texts might make better sense? What happens when the texts are interpreted in the light of the American kinship system?

A second aspect of testing the models presented here is to see whether they help in your interpreting Jesus' parable on divorce. I call it a parable for two reasons: (1) when taken literally, it makes as little sense as "You are the salt of the earth" or "You are the light of the world." Obviously, Christians are not physically and literally salt or light. A parable is a literary form of expression in which the parable author intends something else and something more than what he says, and the hearer has to supply that something else and more. The hearer does this by first imagining what the picture in the parable literally looks like, then asking how the picture fits his or her concrete situation. For example, the parable on the salt of the earth in Matt. 5:13 takes off from the concrete picture of the outdoor Palestinian earth-oven or kiln, called "earth" (see Ps. 12:6; Job 28:5). Fire in such an earth-oven was produced by burning dung. To make the dried dung burn, the bottom of the kiln was faced with flat plates of salt, and the dung itself was sprinkled with salt; the salt served as a chemical agent that helped the dung to burn. However, over time, the heat of the oven causes the salt plates to undergo a chemical reaction which makes the plates impede and stifle the burning of the dung. It is when the salt crystals thus chemically change that they must be thrown out—the salt has lost its saltiness. Note that in Luke's version (Luke 14:34–35), the parable concludes: "It [the salt] is fit neither for the land [i.e., the kiln] nor for the dunghill [i.e., to prepare the fuel]; men throw it away." With this parable, then, the hearer has to imagine the concrete situation of salt being used to make fuel burn and sustain the fire. The something else and something more in the picture is that the Christian is to be like salt, causing fire to flame. What is the fire that the Christian is to facilitate? How, when, and where? It is up to the hearer to decide, pass judgment, and act accordingly. This is what a parable is and how it works. When taken literally, it makes no sense. I believe, as we shall see, that Jesus' statement on divorce is such a parable.

Another reason why I believe it is a parable is that in the Gospels of Matthew and Mark (Luke has it as a one-liner only), this teaching requires further, private explanation, a procedure these authors use for parables. For example, read Mark 4:2–20, with private explanation in vv. 10 ff.; Mark 7:14–23, with private explanation in vv. 17 ff. (See also Matt. 13:3–23; 15:10–20.) The literary form of public teaching in parable and private explanation is the same for the divorce statements in Mark 10:2–12 and Matt. 19:3–12. Along with these two passages from Mark and Matthew, there are three others that contain the tradition of Jesus' teaching of divorce: Matt. 5:31–32; Luke 16:18; and Paul in 1 Cor. 7:10–11.

Of these five passages, which represents as closely as possible what Jesus said? New Testament scholars know that the Gospels present us with what the authors say that the tradition before them said that Jesus said and did. Between the writing of the traditions and Jesus' ministry stand some forty years. Over those years, Jesus' teaching was remembered and applied and reapplied in diverse situations, in circumstances that differed from what Jesus experienced in Palestine before the Roman destruction of Jerusalem in A.D. 70. This means that the traditions about divorce presented in the Gospels are undoubtedly shaped in such a way that they might be useful to the communities of Matthew, Mark, and Luke, while Paul hands on Jesus' teaching on divorce in a way applicable to the people at Corinth.

Relative to this divorce tradition, scholars believe that the original teaching of Jesus is to be found in the first part of Luke 16:18, thus: "Every one who divorces his wife and marries another commits adultery." Now if this is what Jesus said, it has to be a parable. For what does it mean? In line with the kinship norms we have considered, adultery means to trespass on the honor of another male by having sexual intercourse with his wife, who is embedded in the husband. It is something like theft, which is trespassing on the honor of another male by taking some goods which are embedded in that male, the owner. The question Jesus' statement, in the form above, would raise for the first-century man is: How can I, if I divorce my wife, commit adultery, which only some other male can commit against me or I against him, but never against myself? The statement on divorce cited above has the same semantic quality as the statement "Everyone who sells his TV set and buys another is guilty of theft" or "Everyone who gives his child up for adoption and adopts another is guilty of kidnapping." Literally, such statements would make no sense, since in the culture, buying and selling are not theft, and giving up for adoption and adopting are not kidnapping. Similarly, divorcing one's wife and marrying another is not adultery. However, it is important to note that since the time of Hosea (2:18 ff.), the relation of God and His people is depicted in terms of a marriage metaphor, and in terms of this metaphor, adultery is equivalent to idolatry (see Hos. 2:2 ff.; 3:1 ff.; 4:12 ff.; compare also Jer. 2:2; 5:7; 9:2; 13:22–27; Ezek. 16:32–37; 23:37,43,45. In terms of which marriage strategies do these prophets speak?). Passages in the New Testament like Matt. 12:39; 16:4; Mark 8:38; James 4:4 ("unfaithful" in R.S.V. = "adulterous" in Greek); and Rev. 2:20 carry the same metaphoric quality.

Now it is because the statement on divorce makes no sense literally that the Christian tradition in the Pauline and post-Pauline periods (and perhaps earlier) had to interpret the statement to make sense of it and apply it to the social needs of the Christian community.

To begin with, Luke's addition, "and he who marries a woman divorced from her husband commits adultery" (Luke 16:18), points to one line of interpretation. For how could one who marries a divorced woman commit adultery? Only if in some way she were still embedded in her husband, regardless of the divorce procedure. What would such a long-lasting embedding point to? Would marriage be a legal relationship or a blood relationship? In the text of this chapter, we have already seen some indications that marriage was to some extent and in some social contexts considered a blood relationship. With this in mind, consider the following questions:

—Note that it is the statement "What therefore God has joined together, let not man put asunder" in Mark 10:9 that is clarified by the parable on divorce in Mark 10:11–12. On the other hand, in Matthew, it is the parable on divorce (Matt. 19:9) that is clarified by the parable on the eunuchs (castrated males—a dishonor in Mediterrannean culture) in Matt. 19:11–12. Now what in the previous models might make people believe that in marriage God joins two people together? Dyadic personality? Arranged marriages? Marriage as blood relationship? Why is it difficult in our culture to perceive God putting people together in marriage?

—The statement "And the two shall become one. So they are no longer two but one" (Mark 10:8; Matt. 19:5–6) implies what sort of perception of marriage: a legal relationship or a blood relationship? If marriage is a sort of blood relationship, when does the relationship end?

—Paul's statement in Rom. 7:2 ff., "Thus a married woman is bound by law to her husband as long as he lives," implies what sort of perception of marriage: just a legal relationship, or a blood relationship?

—Does Paul's interpretation of the teaching of Jesus on divorce in 1 Cor. 7:10–11 prohibit divorce or remarriage after divorce? Again, what sort of relationship would envison remarriage after divorce as impossible: a legal relationship or a blood relationship?

—Note that Mark's statement of Jesus' teaching on divorce differs from both Matthew and Luke in that he envisions women initiating divorce (Mark 10:12, compare Matt. 5:32; 19:9; Luke 16:18). What sort of cultural situation would Mark have in mind?

—Matthew differs from Mark, Luke, and Paul in that he injects an exceptive clause—except for unchastity (Matt. 5:32; 19:9). In the light of the kinship norms and defensive marriage strategy outlined above, what would unchastity be for a married woman? Would it be a marriage situation that somehow permanently dishonors the male?

—Finally, after you have considered all the texts with Jesus' teaching on divorce presented in the New Testament and listed above, do these texts prohibit divorce or simply remarriage after divorce? Given the defensive marriage strategy of the period and the line of argument in Matt. 19:4–8 and Mark 10:3–9, would the logical outcome be no divorce (period) or no remarriage after divorce? What does divorce mean in the culture—even with no remarriage? Does the text look to individuals or to dyadic personalities and their families?

6

Clean and Unclean:
Understanding Rules of Purity

With this chapter we take a final look at that group of foreigners who people the New Testament, this time considering their concern about and interest in persons and things that are clean or unclean. Certainly this was a central concern in Palestinian Judaism. Jesus directed a parable to this concern, as most New Testament readers know: "Hear me, all of you, and understand: there is nothing outside a man which by going into him can defile him; but the things which come out of a man are what defile him" (Mark 7:14–16). Further, Jesus seems to have observed some of these purity rules, as witnessed by the fact that after he touches a leper (in Mark 1:40–45), and the leper tells people about it, "Jesus could no longer openly enter a town," since he was unclean because of this contact. Then, in response to God in a vision experience, Peter avows: "I have never eaten anything that is common or unclean" (Acts 10:14). He subsequently interprets the vision to mean "I should not call any man common or unclean"—so the vision was not about food at all (Acts 10:28; read the whole passage, 10:1–48). Finally, early Christian groups seem to have been bothered by "questions of food and drink or with regard to a festival or a new moon or a sabbath" (Col. 2:16), as well as particular observances of "days, and months, and seasons, and years" (Gal. 4:10). These sorts of indications point to purity rules. What are purity rules? What do they mean? Why are they of central concern in first-century Judaism? What was the early Christian attitude toward them? To understand these questions, perhaps the best place to begin is with the common human experience called the sacred.

Sacred and Profane

Let me start with a series of examples. Imagine that you are in your favorite department store to buy a new pair of jeans. All of a sudden a little boy walks in, browsing and licking a full ice cream cone. To your surprise, the little boy proceeds to the tables with the jeans on them and carefully rubs his ice cream cone along the seams of the piled clothing, streaking several piles of the expensive pants in this way. What is your reaction when you see this? How do you feel? What will you do? You might laugh, tell the child to stop it, look for his mother, tell a salesperson, or some such thing. But what if you walk into the store, pick up your jeans, pay the salesperson for an expensive pair, and while you are waiting for a receipt and a bag, the little boy runs up and smashes his ice cream cone on your new purchase? Now that the jeans are yours—well fitting and paid for—what is your reaction? The feeling you have for what you have set apart for yourself is a feeling of the sacred; the jeans on the table in the store, not set apart for anyone yet, are profane.

Or imagine that you are studying and all of a sudden hear someone in your vicinity yelling for help. What is your reaction? You might get up, attempt to scare off an intruder, call a security guard or the police. But what if the person being assaulted and screaming for help is your mother, father, sister, or brother? What is your reaction then? How do you feel? The feeling you have for those persons somehow set apart and special to you, your parents, brothers, and sisters, for example, is a feeling of the sacred. Other human beings normally do not get you so emotionally involved when they are in dire straits. After all, you see them on the TV news every day; those others are profane as far as you are concerned.

Or imagine that you see a person dumping some garbage in the middle of the street where you live. What is your reaction? How do you feel about it, even if you are not especially ecology-minded? Now imagine that the person with the garbage walks into your house or dorm and up to your room and proceeds to dump the garbage on your bed. How do you feel about that? The feeling you have for your space—your room and your bed—and its being invaded that way is a feeling of the sacred. What is outside your house, outside your dorm room, what belongs to the public (meaning, in our culture, to no one in particular) is profane and requires a different set of feeling cues.

Finally, imagine that you have worked all semester and are looking forward to a forthcoming vacation to ski, swim, or whatever your favorite vacation pastime happens to be. Then vacation time comes, and you find that your teachers have assigned you all sorts of work, leaving you no vacation time. What is the difference between work time and vacation time? How do you feel about vacation time? How does the feeling differ from your feeling about work time? Our lives are punctuated by breaks in the regular flow of normal time—by vacations for longer stretches of work time, by weekends for shorter stretches. Vacation time, like the weekend, is time set apart, special to you and your purposes; it is sacred time. Work time, regular time like ordinary clock time, is profane.

Now what I want to illustrate by means of these examples is that even in our individualistic, so-called secularized world, we still share in the basic human experience called the sacred. The sacred is that which is set apart to or for some person. It includes persons, places, things, and times that are symboled or filled with some sort of set-apartness which we and others recognize. The sacred is what is mine as opposed to what is yours or theirs, what is ours as opposed to what is yours or theirs. (In our culture, it might be no one's, since we believe in all goods being limitless, but in the first-century world, there is nothing that is no one's—all goods are limited and distributed). Some common synonyms for the sacred include holy, saint, and sacral.

The opposite of the sacred is the profane, the unholy, the non-sacred. The profane is that which is not set apart to or for some person in any exclusive way, that which might be everybody's and nobody's in particular to varying degrees. Thus the words "sacred" and "profane" describe a human relationship of varying degrees of exclusivity relative to some person or thing (and I include time and space under "thing"). For example, to say that human life is sacred is to point out that human life is set apart and exclusive among the forms of life we might encounter, and therefore that it should be treated differently from animal life. Again, to say that sex is sacred means that human sexual encounters are set apart and exclusive among the various forms of sexual encounter we might know, and therefore that human sexual encounters are unlike and not to be treated as animal copulations. These examples derive from a comparison of the human with the animal domain and indicate belief in the exclusivity of the human. To profane human life and behavior is to treat them just like animal life and behavior.

You have undoubtedly noted that delineating self-apartness can take place in different dimensions: between mine and yours, between ours and theirs, and between the human and the non-human. Obviously, other lines can be drawn, and perhaps the set of lines we are most used to are those that mark off the area of persons, things, and events set apart by or for or to God. We often refer to this area as *the* sacred, *the* holy, *the* sacral. We speak of God's holy people—a group of people set apart by or for God or God's service; God's holy name—God's person symboled by his name and belonging to a category that is fully unlike and not to be treated as any human name or person. We also talk of sacrifice, a word that literally means to make (*-fice*) sacred or holy (*sacri-*), hence, to set apart to or for God, the nation, the family, or some other person. The word "sancti-fy" means much the same thing.

The perception of the sacred, of the set apart, clearly implies some sort of social lines marking off one side from the other, animal from human, mine from yours, ours from theirs, God's from ours. You might recall that in the discussion of honor and shame, I began with the observation that human meaning-building is a process of socially contriving lines in the shapeless stuff of the human environment, thus producing definition, socially shared meaning. Human groups draw lines through and around time (the social times of childhood, adulthood, old age) and space (the social spaces called your house and your neighbor's, called our country and Canada). They also mark off persons with social roles and statuses, things with norms of ownership, and God as a unique being controlling the whole human scene.

Human beings the world over are born into systems of lines that mark off, delimit, and define nearly all significant human experiences. Not only do people define and delimit, but they also invest the marked off areas (persons, things, places, events) with feeling, with value. Line-drawing of this sort enables us to define our various experiences so as to situate ourselves and others and everything and everyone that we might come into contact with, as well as to evaluate and feel about those experiences on the basis of where they are located within the lines. Thus the set of social lines we learn through enculturation provides all of us with a sort of socially shared map that helps and compels us to situate persons, things, places, and events. Line-making normally results in a special social emphasis on the boundaries, since clear boundaries mean clear definition, meaning, and feeling, while blurred boundaries lead to ambiguous perceptions and reactions.

Purity: Clean and Unclean

Consequently, social lines are quite necessary for us to perceive set-apartness. Set-apartness relative to persons and the sorts of exclusive relationships between persons and other persons, places, things, and events refers to the experience of the holy, the sacred. However, not all human experiences deal with exclusiveness in relationships. There are things and places and persons which we define, situate, and locate, but with which we have no sort of relationship of exclusiveness. We do not invest ourselves in everything and everybody in the same way we do with our possessions, our parents, brothers and sisters, our special times and places, our God. Yet we do in fact use a set of lines to define, situate, and locate others, even those whom we might never see in a lifetime on this planet, for example, people, places, and things in other parts of our state, country, and world. Now *purity* is specifically about the general cultural map of social time and space, about arrangements within the space thus defined, and especially about the boundaries separating the inside from the outside. The unclean or impure is something that does not fit the space in which it is found, that belongs elsewhere, that causes confusion in the arrangement of the generally accepted social map because it overruns boundaries, and the like. The sacred and profane, then, would be subsets of purity rules dealing with relations of exclusivity. But purity rules in general deal with places and times for everything and everyone, with everyone and everything in its proper place and time. Yet if the arrangements presented in purity rules are exclusive to our group and no other, we might readily consider them sacred purity rules.

Purity rules are much concerned with dirt. Garden dirt in the back yard is in its proper place. When the same dirt gets into the house, the house is considered "dirty," unclean, impure. Dirt is a way of speaking of something out of place. Dirt is a sort of metaphor for matter (and sometimes persons) out of place. It is matter out of place that makes your room dirty. And of course, there are degrees of dirt. For example, you might clean your dorm room for the upcoming visit of your parents, yet when your mother sees the room she invariably says, "This is clean?" She finds dirt where you purified and cleansed. Clean and dirty, then, are matters of degree. But please note one thing here. Wherever people perceive dirt, we can presume that some sort of order exists. Dirt presumes a system, a set of line markings, definition; otherwise one would never know that anything was dirty, unclean, out of place. Further, dirt presumes that persons, places, and things do get out of place, since dirt is matter out of place. In this connection, our society calls people out of place "deviants."

Once persons, places, or things get put in their proper place, put in order, the result is a restoration of the clean and pure. The process of restoring things and people to their places can be called purifying or cleansing. Conversely, the process of putting things and people out of place can be called defiling. Now both defiling and purification presuppose some movement across a symbolic line which marks off the clean from the unclean. Such line-crossing is a sort of transition from the clean to the unclean state, or vice versa. And this transition is across a boundary. As we have previously noted, boundaries are often ambiguous, often a source of anxiety and conflict as well as of satisfaction and fulfillment. For example, graduating from college is a transition, a line-crossing. Some students are happy over the crossing; others feel anxious and unsure. In either case, graduating students go through a social transition, a line-crossing. For the present, please note that between clean and unclean there must be a line.

Anomalies and Abominations

While every culture patterns reality by means of such line-making, yet no culture thoroughly exhausts all the dimensions of human being and human experience, just as no human language makes use of all the sounds human speech organs are capable of producing. Cultures are selective, limited, and limiting. So every culture eventually has to confront experiences that defy its cues, that do not measure up to its assumptions and classifications. Our culture, for example, cues us to perceive other human beings as individualistic personalities, while our first-century foreigners were cued to perceive others as dyadic personalities. What happens when one culture is confronted with the other's prevalent personality type? Our culture cues us to perceive the functioning of human organisms in terms of biological "laws" and to adjust malfunctions of such organisms by means of technological manipulations: when your appendix gets infected, you have someone cut you open and cut it out. Our first-century foreigners were cued to perceive the functioning of human beings in terms of personal causality in significant circumstances, so illness is healed by various interpersonal and non-technological means—for example, an application of olive oil or the laying on of the hands of a healer. They would truly have been impressed by the miracle of modern medicine, just as we tend to disbelieve or wonder about the miracles of their quite usual wonder workers. What I am driving at is that cultures have to deal with realities that do not fit their cues, and every culture eventually faces a larger or lesser number of such realities. These experiences that do not fit socially shared patterns or norms are called anomalies (the word literally means something irregular). If we are enculturated to react with strong negative feelings toward certain anomalies, to view them as triggers of disgust or hate, we would call this class of anomalies *abominations*. For example, we learn that it is proper to get rid of excess matter in the nose by blowing it out into a handkerchief or tissue, then carrying it around with us until we can dispose of it. We find it disgusting if a person bends over and blows his nose on the pavement. This latter type of behavior is an abomination in our culture, perhaps more abominable than killing someone who is trying to steal our TV set.

Be that as it may, cultures do not ignore the anomalies which specific cultural cues dredge up but cannot fit into their patterns. The reason for this is that if anomalies are ignored, people who embody the culture will lose confidence in the cultural cues. For example, our culture cues us to believe all goods are limitless, and this same culture now forces us to face the oil shortage, a case of something not being limitless. We must now fit this limit within our shared belief in limitlessness. If we can, for example by the invention of synthetic fuels, then the system will go well because the limit has been removed and obliterated. But if we cannot fit the anomaly into our system, then we will be forced to adopt living arrangements that are limited—and there goes the American way. Similarly, in the first century, believing Jews knew they were God's people, living in God's land, and worshiping a God of power who was capable of everything. What an anomaly it must have been to have the land occupied by the Romans and their gods! The longer the occupation, the more urgent became the problem of reconciling God's power and abilities in the face of the anomalous unbeliever and his god's power. Unless such a major anomaly were reconciled, the cultural system would run down or be radically changed.

So every culture must have some ways for dealing with anomalies or abominations that fall between the cracks of its boundaries or lie outside its classification system. There are at least five ways of facing up to anomalies. *First,* elites or opinion leaders can settle for one interpretation of life, thus reducing ambiguity and eliminating anomalies from attention. For example, we can settle for a belief in a mechanistic, technological view of reality, and thus anything supernatural would be classified as superstition, hallucination, error, insanity, or heresy. Early Christianity got rid of dissenting interpretations of the experience of Jesus by settling upon a canon or collection of normative writings—our New Testament. This collection sustains a single range of interpretation of Jesus, with all other interpretations considered erroneous, heresy. Judaism settled for one range of interpretation of marriage relations, with all others ranked unclean or abominations. *Second,* any anomaly might be controlled physically. For example, people in our society who commit murder are generally physically removed from our midst. Criminal Roman elites were exiled or banished, thus physically removed from their society. Judaism had certain classes of people removed to the peripheries of their towns and cities, like those afflicted with certain types of skin disease (notably psoriasis, which our translations give as "leprosy"; Hansen's disease was rare or non-existent in the Middle East during biblical times). *Third,* society might impose strict and clearly spelled out rules for avoiding anomalous persons, things, and behavior. Such rules affirm and strengthen what is socially unacceptable and indirectly underscore what is acceptable. For example, our belief that smoking causes cancer is being worked out in rules for avoiding smoke, and hence smokers are confined to certain places, even though we believe in individualism to such an extent that a minor female or a married female needs no one's consent to have an abortion. The smoke avoidance rules affirm what is socially unacceptable and indirectly underline what is acceptable. Roman citizens were forbidden to marry slaves, thus maintaining boundaries between classes and indirectly highlighting the rank of citizen. Jewish food prohibitions imply a list of foods that are to be positively favored. *Fourth,* the anomalous person, thing, or event can be labeled as a public hazard, thus putting the anomaly beyond discussion and furthering conformity. For example, the Three Mile Island nuclear plant broke down and subsequently was officially labeled a public hazard. Such a label makes discussion of the benefits of nuclear energy in Pennsylvania beside the point and aids in forming opinion against nuclear energy. By labeling Judaism and Christianity "atheist," that is, lacking belief in the traditional gods of the Romans, Roman leaders put any discussion of Christianity and Judaism outside the realm of possibility and thus furthered conformity in rejecting them. By labeling Jesus' healing activity as the work of Beelzebul, Jesus opponents try to make it highly unlikely that anyone would take him seriously, thus helping generate conformity in rejecting him.

Fifth, anomalies can be used in ritual to enrich meaning or call attention to other levels of existence. Thus violence—an anomaly in our law-and-order society—can be used in our national ritual of football. It can also be used to remind us of the violence we must do to ourselves to lead a good life, or how hard we must compete to make it in the economic rat race. Jesus drives out a demon named Legion (an allusion to the Roman occupying forces) and sends the multiple demon into a herd of swine (a perpetually unclean, abominable creature in Jewish perception), thus calling attention to the relationship of the demon to the Romans to the abominable. Undoubtedly you can think of more examples that might fit these categories. A whole series of them might be found in ordinary college bull sessions about science and religion—science here meaning technology, as it ordinarily does among college students and not a few of their teachers. Religions imported into the United States (like Christianity and Judaism) provide a host of anomalies that do not fit the technological paradigm, while technology provides a large number of anomalies that cannot fit religions of other cultures.

Be that as it may, purity rules deal with system and order, with definitions of general boundaries and of exclusivity, with the anomalies that simply defy classification or that are positively abominations. Every culture has such purity rules, for every culture has a classification system. Yet cultures adopt different emphases, perspectives, or horizons in developing their classification systems. Our culture is poised on an individualistic horizon of limitless good attained by the individual's mastery of the social and natural environment, hence by means of social and physical technology, like ten rules to manipulate another to get him or her on a date, or five rules to follow to get better gas mileage. From this horizon, we get a set of rules, of classifications, that differs notably from first-century Palestine, which was pivoted on dyadic personality and the perspective of limited good to be maintained by interpersonal competence in line with honor and shame.

Furthermore, since purity rules present a sort of grid that covers all aspects of society, such rules are equally concerned with maintaining the wholeness or completeness of the social body. The pure social body is much like a perfect container with no overflow or oozing in or out, a complete body. From this perspective, purity rules are very concerned with the outer borders of the society and strive to maintain society's integrity or wholeness.

For example, note our interest in illegal aliens, passports, visas, health certificates, and the like. As I mentioned previously, purity rules have a place for everything and everyone, with everything and everyone in its place—and with anomalies properly excluded. And just as society as a whole is a social body defined by purity rules, so also is the individual. The individual in a given society is a personal body defined by purity rules which replicate the societal rules and fit the individual into the social body. In other words, the individual human being can be considered a sort of portable road map of the terrain and features that mark and define the larger social world. Thus the individual, too, will be concerned about wholeness and completeness, about being a perfect entity with no overflow or oozing in or out, hence with individual completeness. For example, note our zeal in curbing offensive odors in the individual with mouthwashes, deodorants, scented soaps, and the like, that keep odors from the borders of others and within our own. Finally, since God-talk, or theology, necessarily consists in comparisons drawn from human experience, God, too, will be described in terms of the concerns of society and of the individual in the society. God will be described as complete, whole, perfect, and this perfection will be discernible in God's relationship to his people, his world.

The common perception is that observance of purity rules brings prosperity both to the society and to the individuals in that society, while infringement brings danger. In our society, the main purity rules concern the symbol called money, with health running a close second. Money is a quantitative line marker serving as norm for social status; it enables the pursuit of individualistic happiness within those statuses that we consider significant. Health is individualistic, technological health (the body as a sort of mechanical organism is viewed technologically). Health marks the ability of the individual to function productively within society as a whole and within his or her own status in particular. You might note that the only forms of segregation and discrimination permitted in the United States (hence, the only overt boundary markers) are those deriving from money and health. You can live wherever you want, eat and buy whatever you want, regardless of who you are, provided that you have the money. If you lack the money, you are in effect segregated from those who have it, hence you are in a lower class. Similarly, you are considered a possible productive member of society when you are physically and emotionally capable of acting as an individual, individualistically. Adults who are physically or emotionally dependent upon others are generally considered unclean, unable to respect societal lines. On the other hand, those who are a threat to the money or health of the moneyed or healthy are abominations, deviants. Deviants get excluded from ordinary social intercourse, while normal folks who find themselves in an unclean state by means of crossing boundaries into areas where they ought not be (e.g., breaking a parking law, infringing on your neighbors' rights to privacy) have to be purified and cleansed, normally with money (fines, fees, and so on).

In the limited-good perspective of our first-century foreigners, the main task in life was not symboled by achievement in terms of money, but rather by the maintenance of one's inherited position in society. This brought prosperity and insured the most harmonious relationship possible in terms of time, place, interpersonal relationships with one's fellows, and relationships with God. This kind of prosperity was the task of the dyadic personality as well as of his society as a whole. The purity rules of the society were intended to foster prosperity by maintaining fitting, harmonious relationships. Thus perfection—the wholeness marked off by purity rules—characterizes God, the people in general, and the individual. This perfection gets spelled out in replicating patterns (recall that replication means the same rules in different areas), perhaps most apparent in the categories of persons and their interaction in marriage, in temple worship, as well as in the fellowship of the meal. Before we consider Jesus' reaction to Jewish purity laws, it is obviously necessary to have some idea of what those rules were and how they outfitted society with meaning.

A Classification of Persons in Judaism

After our discussion of kinship and marriage in first-century Palestine, we know that the defensive marriage strategy of Judaism required marriage partners to come from within the covenant community. However, as we might expect from a limited-good society, this Jewish covenant community was highly stratified into categories of persons who received their place by birth. Genealogical purity, the lines defining one's inherited status within the defensive community, was certainly a major concern of the elites, and perhaps of the non-elites as well. In Ezra 2:2–58 and Neh. 7:7–60, we find a simple classification of the population in terms of degrees of purity deriving from proximity to the Jerusalem Temple, which was a large area of courts and buildings with the central pivotal locus being the sanctuary, the holy of holies. From the viewpoint of the kinship system and the defensive approach to life, since the whole genealogical community is perceived as God-given, its genealogical purity lines are considered to be God's will for his people. The promises of the age to come hold for the people, the offspring of Abraham, to the degree of their God-appointed purity. According to early rabbinic traditions, which probably mirror the situation during New Testament times (cited from

Joachim Jeremias, *Jerusalem in the Time of Jesus*, p. 271 ff. and conflated), the genealogical categories of persons one might find in Palestine—from a Jewish perspective—included the following:

a   1. Priests

b   2. Levites

c   3. Full-blooded Israelites ("laymen")

       4. Illegal children of priests

d   5. Proselytes or Gentile converts to Judaism

       6. Proselytes who once were slaves, hence proselyte freedmen

       7. Bastards (those born of incestuous or adulterous unions)

       8. The "fatherless" (those born of prostitutes)

e   9. Foundlings

      10. Eunuchs made so by men

      11. Eunuchs born that way

f   12. Those of deformed sexual features

      13. Hermaphrodites

x   14. Gentiles, i.e., non-Jews

What is the basis of this set of categories? You will remember that in defensive marriage strategy, it is imperative to intermarry solely with those belonging to the covenant community—and within one's social class, if possible. Hence potential marriage partners must be members of the covenant group by birth or by ritual birth (converts, called proselytes) and occupy a given social class. Further, the defensive strategy calls for holy seed, hence offspring exclusive to God because born of parents respecting God's rules for his holy people. Thus the person marrying must be capable of having children, thereby transmitting his own inherited status—inheritance of status follows the father. Therefore, the criteria for fitting into the purity lines of this group include covenant membership and capacity to procreate. Further, this defensive community possessed a fundamental, overt class structure based on birth: priest, Levite, and layman or full Israelite. Thus covenant membership likewise implied inherited status.

The marriage rules, that is, purity rules applied to marriage, were obviously the work of the preindustrial city elites. They went as follows:

1) True Israel consisted specifically of priests, Levites, and full-blooded laymen (categories a,b,c). These persons were genealogically clean, with proper pedigrees. They could all freely intermarry.

2) Proselytes and proselyte freedmen were ranked separately, since they might be said to bear a slight genealogical doubt. Along with them were included the illegal children of priests. These latter were not illegitimate, but

rather children of priests who married prohibited women like widows, divorcees, or seduced women (see Lev. 21:7). Technically, a priest must always marry a female of true Israelite pedigree, unused or untouched by any other male; otherwise, his offspring are ranked with proselytes. Persons in this category (d) did in fact belong to Israel and could marry Levites and full Israelites, but never priests. Hence they were clean for some Israelites, unclean for others.

3) Category (e): Bastards, the fatherless, foundlings, and eunuchs had a grave genealogical impediment about them: they were simply not whole and complete. They could not properly trace their ancestry, might derive from highly disreputable ancestors, and in the case of the eunuch, could no longer transmit covenant status. These persons do not possess *both* covenant membership by birth and the capability of transmitting the status of proper covenant membership. They might possess one feature or the other, but not both. These could intermarry or even marry proselytes, but they were forbidden to marry priests, Levites, full Israelites, and the illegal children of priests—the group functionally forming "true Israel" and intimately bound up with the Temple.

4) Category (f): Eunuchs from birth, those of deformed sexual features, and hermaphrodites could not marry at all. They were incapable of sexual relations, hence incapable of transmitting covenant status.

5) Category (x): The Gentiles were an abomination, simply off the purity scale altogether.

If we view these inherited statuses and the permissible defensive marriage interactions in terms of a Venn diagram, the picture would look as follows:

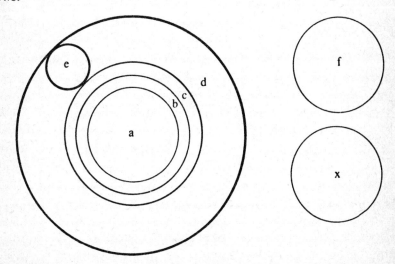

The categories derive from proximity to the Temple (and its holy place)—priest, Levite, layman—along with two qualities: being a member of the covenant community by birth or ritual birth, and the capacity to transmit one's status within the covenant community:

x: abomination: off the purity scale entirely, hence necessarily unclean

f: always unclean for marriage since they cannot fit the criteria for inclusion on the purity scale

d: Israel, including those by ritual birth (proselytes). Some in this category are capable of marrying into "true" Israel at the Levite and Israelite level, but not at the priest level, hence they are clean for some, unclean for others in the inner circles.

c: those who are Israelite by birth, "true" Israel, but among these there is a special category (b)

b: Levites: these persons are fit for Temple service, but lack the qualities to fit them into category (a)

a: priests: fit both for the Temple and for the altar (holy place)

e: those of (d) who either fit dubiously under the covenant or have a questionable inherited status to transmit or cannot transmit it any longer.

These categories of persons in first-century Palestine represent an abstract model of the purity lines of Judaism, a symbolic statement of who is allowed to enter the social body of Israel. Entrance is by birth, and circumcision marks the rite of entry. It should come as no surprise if we find that the classification of clean and unclean animals—what in the realm of animals is allowed to enter the individual body of the Israelite or the worshiping body at the Temple—closely fits these categories of persons. This would be another instance of replication: the same rules in another dimension.

Classification of Clean and Unclean Animals

In fact, much as the holy land is holy because it belongs to God, so is all Israel along with Israel's domestic animals. This parallel between Israel and its domestic beasts can be seen in the fact that the first-born, "the first to open the womb among the people of Israel, both of man and of beast," is the Lord's (Exod. 13:2; 22:29b–30; Lev. 27:26–27; Num. 3:13; 8:17–18; 18:15), as well as in the fact that temple sacrifices are to come only "from the herd or from the flock" (Lev. 1:2), that is, from domestic animals. Domestic animals are to observe the sabbath, just like their owners and masters (Exod. 20:8–11; Deut. 5:12–15; for the sabbath year, Lev. 25:6–7). Finally, just as Israel is to avoid marriage with Gentiles—as though Gentiles formed another species—so too the crossbreeding of domestic animals of different species is forbidden (Lev. 19:19).

By replication, the categories that divide one class of Israelites from another in the marriage purity rules will divide their animals. However, there are non-domestic animals in the holy land as well, and these too must be patterned to make sense of the total environment. This is precisely where the categories of clean and unclean in Leviticus 11 fit in. These categories cover all the animals of the environment: water, air, and land creatures. The replication of marriage purity rules mainly looks to land creatures, as we shall see. At present, consider Leviticus 11.

The categories of Leviticus 11 cover all the animals of the environment, with only the domestic variety fit for the Temple. The animals are divided, first of all, according to their habitats: water, air, or land. The anomalous are rejected immediately; they are an abomination because they fall outside the categories. For example, amphibians that live between two spheres and in both (Lev. 11:10). Then specific criteria for each category are spelled out: proper land animals are "whatever parts the hoof and is cloven-footed and chews the cud" (Lev. 11:3): The proper water animal is "everything in the waters that has fins and scales" (Lev. 11:9). Finally, proper air animals are those that do not eat blood and carrion, can fly or hop with their wings and two legs (like the locust: Lev. 11:13–22).

Anomalies in these categories include any creatures having the defining features of members of another category, like land animals that swarm like fish or insects (Lev. 11:29 ff.), winged creatures that go on all fours like land animals (the insects, Lev. 11:20), or creatures lacking in the main defining features (e.g., crabs and eels are water creatures lacking fins and scales). However, creeping, crawling and/or swarming and teeming creatures lack criteria for allocation into any one class, since there are animals in all three areas that behave this way. Thus "every swarming thing that swarms upon the earth is an abomination; . . . Whatever goes on its belly, and whatever goes on all fours, or whatever has many feet, all the swarming things that swarm upon the earth, you shall not eat; for they are an abomination" (Lev. 11:41–42). Now for purposes of comparison with the previous classification of persons, consider the following Venn diagram of land creatures (taken from Mary Douglas):

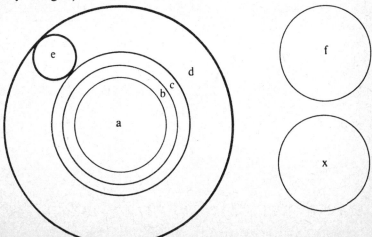

The categories, like those for persons, derive from proximity to the Temple (and the altar) along with two qualities: domestication and cud-chewing, parted-hoofed features.

x: abomination: any land animal that swarms is off the purity scale entirely, hence necessarily unclean.

f: always unclean for table use, since they cannot fit the criteria for inclusion on the purity scale. These have neither cloven hoofs nor chew the cud, are not domesticated, and they would include predators and carrion-eaters like lions, bears, foxes, and dogs (which were not pets in the ancient Near East).

d: animals of the land of Israel that are domesticated or not domesticated, but have cloven hoofs or chew the cud or both. These can be clean or unclean for table use

c: those animals which have parted hoofs and chew the cud are clean and fit for table use (Lev. 11:3; Deut. 14:4–6 for non-domesticated). Among these there is a special category (b).

b: unblemished clean animals of domestic herds and flocks; these are fit for the altar (Lev. 22:20 for the general rule), unless an added requirement is demanded (e.g., Lev. 1:3, 10; 4:3, 23, 28; 5:15, 18).

a: unblemished clean animals of domestic herds and flocks fit for the altar with added requirement of age (e.g., a year old—Lev. 9:3; 23:18) or quality (e.g., all first-born are to be given to the priest [Num. 18:15]).

e: those of (d) that do not *both* have cloven hoofs and chew the cud, i.e., do one or the other but not both, even when domesticated (Lev. 11:4–7). The pig is listed here quite neutrally, but in the second century B.C. becomes an especially unclean animal because of its use as sacred animal by Gentiles, notably from the Maccabean period on (see 1 Macc. 1:41–64 and 2 Macc. 6:4–5).

Thus, as Mary Douglas has pointed out, we find a parallel set of purity lines marking off Israel and its animals. These might be summarized as follows:

Israelites: Their animals:

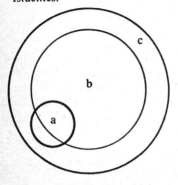
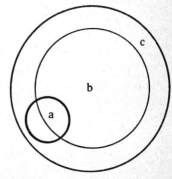

c: all who are under the covenant, clean and unclean—but never abominable

b: fit for Temple worship or sacrifice: only the clean without blemish

a: consecrated to the Temple: first-born without blemish, of men and beasts (read Lev. 21:17–23; 27:26–27; Exod. 13:2, 11–16; 22:29–30).

Relative to category (b) above, those fit for Temple worship or sacrifice, our previous classification of persons dealt only with their clean or unclean state relative to birth. Birth marks only the beginning of a process in which the individual has further occasion to be blemished or rendered unclean, hence unfit for social intercourse with his fellows in various degrees, running in concentric circles from the central hub, the Temple. For example, Lev. 12—15 lists those who are unclean and must withdraw from social relations with their fellows. These include persons suffering from skin disorders or unusual, abnormal bodily flows like menstruation, seminal emission, suppuration. In these instances the personal boundaries of the individual are afflicted; the individual is not whole. The same holds for contact with a cadaver. Further, a blemished priest or layman was not allowed to offer sacrifice: "For no one who has a blemish shall draw near, a man blind or lame, or one who has a mutilated face or a limb too long, or a man who has an injured foot or an injured hand, or a hunchback, or a dwarf, or a man with a defect in his sight or an itching disease or scabs or crushed testicles" (Lev. 21:18–20). In these cases, the persons described likewise are not whole. The unclean and the blemished simply cannot symbol wholeness, perfection, and hence they cannot replicate the ideal: the perfect individual in the perfect society under the perfect God.

Now that we have some idea of how persons fit into their proper places, and how animals replicate persons and fit into their proper places, we will turn to the process by which persons and their animals symbolically interact with God. This process is called sacrifice, in this case meaning an offering holy to and for God. At bottom, such an offering is the process of making something sacred to another.

Sacrifice: The Process of Holy Offering

At the beginning of this chapter, I set out a number of examples pointing to how we experience the sacred in terms of what we consider exclusively set aside for ourselves. Recall the jeans in the first example. How did the jeans get set apart to or for you? The process, which we might call buying or purchasing, has three abstract steps to it. At the beginning the jeans are rooted in their normal merchandising position, the property of some impersonal corporation like the manufacturing company or the department store. As you start making your selection, you set some jeans apart from this normal state as you try them on, consider their qualities, and the like. And as your interest in a particular pair grows, you consider them as possibly yours, as not exactly the same as all the rest on the tables or racks, and you would be offended if another customer came and took them from your hands—even though they are not yet yours. The jeans as a possible purchase, as potentially yours, are in a middle phase, separated from the merchandiser's pile, but not yet yours. This is a sort of boundary or marginal state. To help you through the marginal state, you get yourself a ceremonial leader, a salesperson, who runs through a ceremony or rite by means of which the marginal jeans are passed on to a new status: they become yours, set apart to or for you. They become sanctified to or for you. This little rite of sanctification, then, consists of three phases which might be depicted as follows:

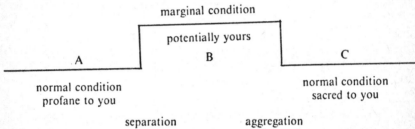

This sort of process can be discerned in our dealings with many things. However, it also underlies the significant social changes that persons undergo. For example, your movement in the marginal condition called college is toward a new sort of sacred state, a profession of life career. You began this movement from a normal condition of being qualified for nothing in particular. Similarly, getting married is a sort of process from the normal condition of being unmarried through a marginal condition of decision, planning, and rite, to a new normal condition of being married. In the first phase, potential mates are profane to each other; in the second phase they become potentially sacred to each other and eventually go through some sort of ceremony or rite that realizes the mutual setting apart. The result is the new normal state of being holy to or for each other, being married. Note that both through college and in getting married, there are ceremonial leaders, socially acknowledged, who bring you through the marginal condition.

This description is temporal since it looks at the process in terms of time. However, we can also depict the process from the viewpoint of space. Relative to things, you already own a number of things in a spatial sphere which we might call your sacred area. Then there is obviously an enormous amount of things outside your sacred area which are not yours, which are profane to you. Finally, there is the overlapping area where you interact with the profane and acquire new items that become sacred to and for you, a sort of spatial marginal area. Spatially, the arrangement would look as follows:

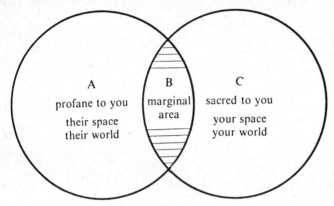

A
profane to you
their space
their world

B
marginal
area

C
sacred to you
your space
your world

The way you set apart or sanctify things is by moving them from their world (or nobody's world in our limitless-good culture) to your world. Your world, including the persons and things in that world, are sacred to you. You shaped and acquired your world because your parents introduced you into your world (which was their world with you as outsider) from the marginal area of birth. At this marginal area, they could either accept or reject you, and in this sense there is little difference between being born to or adopted by a given set of parents: in either case they have to choose to accept their child.

Now take the time to apply these two models of space and time to the relationship of man to God. From the viewpoint of time, what is the process of setting apart to God like? From the viewpoint of space, how do the areas of God and man intersect? In first-century Judaism, the space of God was symboled by the Temple, which replicated both the entire holy land and the whole world, like a set of Chinese boxes within each other. The process of setting persons and things apart to or for God is called sanctification, holy-ing, or hallowing (as in "hallowed be thy name"). The process of interacting with God by means of persons and things thus set apart is called sacrifice. The purity rules of our first-century foreigners point to the categories of persons and things and their proper condition and location for taking part in this God-man interaction—in the Temple, in the holy land, and in the world at large. Such rules also replicate in the division of time throughout the year, which covers Temple time, time in the holy land in terms of a week punctuated by sabbath rest, and the broader annual time, punctuated by special feast days. Temple time, sabbath time, and feast-day time are all marginal times, transition times, times when you can ignore your watch, much as you do when you are at a party that you really enjoy or when you are in love or on a fantastic vacation. Watch time makes little sense in

those circumstances, much as focusing on everyday routine matters makes
little sense at parties, on dates, or on vacations. Such times are holy times
and require a different set of focuses.

To get back to our foreigners, consider the spatial arrangement, the holy
spatial lines, of the Jerusalem Temple in the first century. That Temple, much
like Christian churches and shrines the world over, consisted of three general
areas: A) a place where properly prepared persons can assemble; C) a place
marking God's space the sanctuary proper, like the altar located against a far
wall in some Christian churches; B) an intermediate space where interaction
can take place. Of course these general areas can be and are subdivided, but
for starters, take the overall view. The areas would thus correspond to the
circles of space that is yours and not yours, depicted above. However, for
greater exactness, I will surround both circles with a line that embraces persons
not belonging to God's people, hence not fazed by the interaction:

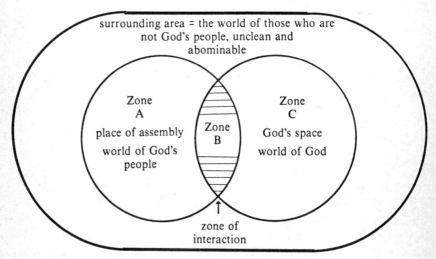

The Temple arrangement replicates that of the holy land in which it is
situated. The Temple is found in Jerusalem, on one of the three hills called
the Temple mount in the first century. Now just as the holy land is God's
land relative to the world created by Him, so Jerusalem is God's city (Matt.
4:5; 27:53) relative to the holy land, and the Temple mount is God's special
mountain relative to the city of Jerusalem. Finally, the sanctuary building
(Matt. 24:15; 1 Cor. 3:17) in the Temple area is God's space relative to the
Temple area in general. Again, we have a set of Chinese boxes that divide up
space to fill it with meaning by reference to a center. In each case the
problem area, the area of anxiety and concern as well as of joy and emotional
highs, is the area of interaction, the margin or borderline. A Jew coming

from abroad is happy to see the holy land; on pilgrimage he is happy to see Jerusalem on the horizon; as worshiper he is overjoyed to see the Temple mount; and as sacrificer he gets high when in the place of assembly he sees the altar and the sanctuary behind it. On the way to Jerusalem, hitting the margins causes emotional response. For an unclean person, a person not allowed at the margins, a sort of reverse experience might be expected. And in the face of a conquering horde, anxiety would mount as margin after margin, limit after limit was crossed over in a march of desecration, of defilement, of reducing everything to the profane. This is how margins, definitions, and limits of purity work in human experience, ours as well as theirs (and I might note, incidentally that they work on the individual body just as they do on the social body).

As we know, Israel believed that its margins, its purity lines, were God-given and God-willed. Relative to the Temple area, we might depict the space vertically as follows (texts describing Solomon's Temple are: Exod. 25—27—even though it is said to take place in the wilderness; Ezek. 40—43—this future Temple is based on recollections of Solomon's temple; and for Herod's first-century Temple, known as the Second Temple, based on biblical regulations and later practice, see Joachim Jeremias, *Jerusalem in the Time of Jesus,* pp. 79–82 for early Jewish sources):

Symbolic space category	*O.T. category*	*1st century*

mixed nature:
    clean, unclean,
    and abominations
	outside the camp	outside the
		    holy land

mixed culture:
    clean or unclean,
    but no abominations
	inside the camp	in the holy land
		    replicated by
		    Jerusalem,
		    the holy city

zone A:
    space of God's
people:
    assembly space
	court of tent	Temple mount
		    and courts of
		a. Gentiles (strangers and
		    sojourners in the land)
		b. (Israelite) women
		c. Israelites

threshold of God's space zone B: space of interaction final limits of man's space	altar and laver table and seven-branched candlestick curtain before the sanctuary	
zone C: God's space	tent with ark holy of holies	porch holy place holy of holies

In this arrangement, the holy of holies marks the center of the Temple mount, which marks the center of Jerusalem, which marks the center of the holy land, which marks the center of the world. At the center of centers, God's holy people have the opportunity to interact with him under the ceremonial direction of God's priests aided by their Levites.

Now why would someone want to interact with God at the Temple? Another way to put that question is: What is the purpose of sacrifice? We already know that we are dealing with dyadic personalities who sought out patrons from higher social strata to help them in maintaining their assigned and inherited social status. In this perspective, the God of Israel occupies the highest conceivable social status, and he invites his people to interact with him. He does not need their sacrifices; rather, they need to sacrifice to him. Why? To enjoy the benefits of God's patronage, which include God's power as well as the joy of God's presence. Sacrifices to God are analogous to gifts given to higher class patrons. What patrons want of their clients is recognition of honor, submission, a following. Sacrifice to God symbols a gift of client to patron, an expression of asymmetrical but reciprocal relationship with a view to power, protection, and the joy of bathing in the presence of the patron of patrons. In Temple sacrifice the offered object—something prescribed and clean—stands for the offerer, who likewise must be clean and unblemished. The object is taken by the ritual leader of the intermediate or marginal zone, who acts as a bridge between the donor's space and the space of God, space that symbols their worlds. By means of this bridge and the activity in the marginal zone, the benefits of the patron pass to the donor, who may be an individual, a group, or the nation at large. In this way sacrifice symbols an interaction between man and God across the marginal or transitional zone. As a rule, after it passes to the marginal zone most of the food offered in sacrifice is eaten by the offerer, his entourage, and the Temple personnel. The transformation of the portions burned at the altar symbolizes passage of the donor to God. The fellowship of the Temple meal clearly symbols the fellowship of a benign patron with his clients. The purpose of it all is clearly religious in the first-century sense of the word, that is, a recognition of the preeminence of God above all social statuses, the admission that God is the one who controls all—hence a broad symbol of honor, submission, and obedience of the donor to God, along with God's acceptance of the donor as client.

In summary, the foregoing models of clean and unclean persons on the basis of birth, of clean and unclean animals somewhat replicating personal categories, of sacred and profane space, and of procedures to cross boundaries all seem to have been in vogue during the lifetime of Jesus. Such purity rules formed the implicit and explicit lines by means of which persons and things were situated in Judaism. However, not long after the death and resurrection of Jesus, a notable group of Christians rejected those purity arrangements. To a Jew this clearly meant a rejection of God's will, of an order ordained by God for patron-client interaction. And with the destruction of the Jerusalem Temple in A.D. 70—after which most of our Gospel documents were written—the sacred center of centers ceases to mark off sacred space as previously, thus vindicating those Christians, like Paul and his followers, who ceased observing Jewish purity rules before A.D. 70.

Christian Purity Arrangements

If we stick to the earliest traditions in the Gospels, we find it to be quite certain that Jesus healed and taught. His healing frequently looked to persons who, in terms of purity rules were blemished, hence either incapable of social relations with the rest of the holy people of Israel (like lepers, Mark 1:40–45; Luke 17:11–19; the woman with a hemorrhage, Mark 5:25–34) or barred from the Temple and sacrifice because of some sort of permanent impediment or lack of wholeness (like those possessed, the paralyzed, the lame, the blind). And these healings are frequently linked with the role and function of sacred time, notably the sabbath (e.g., Mark 1:21–27; 3:1–6; Matt. 12:1–14). By healing on a sabbath, Jesus provokes debate about the meaning of the sabbath—hence about the meaning of purity rules applied to time. This, of course, would imply questions of the meaning of purity rules applied to space and persons as well, since such rules replicate each other, and an alteration in one set requires alterations in the others.

In these debates, Jesus accepts the system of lines set out in the purity rules of the Old Testament, much as he assumes the defensive marriage strategy typical of post-exilic Judaism. But what he seems to question is the general social purpose of these rules and the way they are interpreted in line with this purpose. Their purpose is not to lop off ever greater portions of God's people from access to God, symboled by the clean and the sacred of the purity rules (thus constricting or diminishing zone A in the figures above). Rather, they are to facilitate access to God. The purity rules are to make this access easier, not close it off. Another way to say this is: "The sabbath was made for man, not man for the sabbath" (Mark 2:27).

Furthermore, just as God really has no need of sacrifices, so too God does not need purity rules to confine and hedge him in from the dishonor and outrage of men. God is perfect because he is open to all Israelites, both the good and the bad. Relative to his people in his holy land, "he makes his sun rise on the evil and on the good, and sends rain on the just and on the unjust" (Matt. 5:45). Since God is open to all his people, to do his will is to be open to one's fellow Israelites, whether good or bad, just as God is open to them. God's will, then, is the welfare of his people, and any interpretation of the purity rules should be in the direction of man's welfare, not in the direction of simply maintaining the system in some mechanical way—at the level of hands and feet only. The purpose, the heart, must enter the picture. For example: "Moses said, 'Honor your father and your mother'; and, 'He who speaks evil of father or mother, let him surely die'; but you say, 'If a man tells his father or his mother, What you would have gained from me is Corban' (that is, given to God)—then you no longer permit him to do anything for his father or mother" (Mark 7:10–12; also Matt. 15:4–6, where God commands respect for parents, not Moses). Jesus' contention is that this sort of interpretation, with parents' rights being irreversibly overruled by a person's decision for God and the Temple, indicates lopsided priorities. The same holds for priorities in Temple sacrifice: "So if you are offering your gift at the altar, and there remember that your brother [fellow Israelite] has something against you, leave your gift there before the altar and go; first be reconciled to your brother, and then come and offer your gift" (Matt. 5:23–24). Consequently, if purity rules are to facilitate access to God, and if the God to whom one wants access has man's welfare as the main priority in his will for his people, it follows that proper interpretation of purity rules must derive from giving primary consideration to relationships with one's fellows. This is what righteousness is about. For righteousness means proper interpersonal relationships with all those in one's society, between God and man and between man and man. In the righteousness symboled by Jesus, proper God and man relationships—which are extremely necessary, as the purity rules indicate—require prior proper man and man relationships. Otherwise, the God-man relationship remains at the level of the hands and feet, of activity alone, without the substance of the whole person. This sort of action, without the heart in it, is called formalism. Thus, in the interpretation of the parable on clean and unclean (Mark 7:14–23), "what comes out of a man is what defiles a man." And note that the evil intentions generated by the heart refer to interpersonal relationships that do harm to one's fellows: "For from within, out of the heart of man, come evil thoughts, fornication, theft, murder, adultery, coveting, wickedness, deceit, licentiousness, envy, slander, pride, foolishness."

Thus, while Jesus shares his opponents' view of the symbolic value of the purity rules of the Bible, his activity and teaching point to a new vision of priorities based upon Jesus' own perception of God and God's will. The purity rules, while important, are not central but peripheral to some other central concern. The emphasis ought not to be on how Israel should approach God, but on how God in fact approaches Israel. The purpose of interaction with God (in zone B in the figures above) is to replicate and reveal how God acts toward his people (openness to all, openhanded and openhearted), not to replicate and support how Israel has acted toward God in the past (selective defensiveness developed in traditioning the past). In his activity, Jesus focused upon those in Israel who for some reason or other could not fit into the assembly of God's people (zone A in the figures above). He thus insists upon a similar focus as priority for proper relationship with God. Such an interpretation, of course, tends to displace the Old Testament as God's *priestly* Torah, God's instruction sanctioned as law by the ruling elites of the day, in favor of taking the Old Testament as God's *people* Torah, God's instruction as clarified by his ongoing, present activity among and for his people.

What results is the embedding of the purity rules of the Torah within the Torah as a whole instead of fitting the Torah as a whole into the purity rules, as the elites would insist. Thus interaction with God takes place on the basis of Torah—including Temple sacrifice and purity rules as subsets of the Torah—and not on the basis of God's space confined to the Jerusalem Temple and mediated by priests alone. This would look as follows:

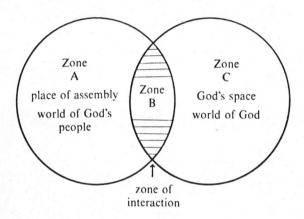

zone of
interaction

God's space is wherever God chooses to reveal himself, wherever people strive to obey and honor God in line with his Torah. The place of assembly is wherever God's people gather to obey and honor him. Such an approach would look quaint to the urban elites. It rather smacks of the prophetism of old with its emphasis on mercy and on loving one's neighbor as oneself as highest ranking priorities, with sacrifice running second (Matt. 9:13; Mark 12:33; Hos. 6:6; Mic. 6:6–8). Certainly some of the non-elites of Jesus' day and age shared these priorities, notably the scribes of the Pharisees. With the fall of Jerusalem and the demise of the urban elites, the Pharisaic scribes do in fact gain the upper hand and implement a program much like that envisioned by Jesus.

However, at an earlier period, in the A.D. thirties, Jesus' followers launch a program of their own. For these followers the resurrection of Jesus meant that Jesus indeed was right in his assessment of the Torah and its implications, since God himself indicated his approval of Jesus by raising him from the dead. If Jesus is right and God's will is man's welfare coupled with purity rules that should symbol ready access to God, then it is no longer "in Israel" that people should seek this access, but "in Christ," and Jesus of Nazareth is this Christ. He himself is indication of God's ongoing activity, hence he supercedes the Torah as law indicating what pleases God. Instead of a Torah-centric being in Israel, early Christianity developed a Christocentric being "in Christ" (Christ occupying zone B).

The first Christian problems seem to have dealt with how in fact a person gets "in Christ." Must one first get "in Israel" or not? So long as Christianity was confined to Israel, that was no problem, of course. But what of Gentiles who wanted to join the Christian group? Must they accept the beliefs of Jesus if they came to believe in Jesus? "Some believers who belonged to the party of the Pharisees rose up, and said, 'It is necessary to circumcise them, and to charge them to keep the law of Moses'" (Acts 15:5). To this approach the Jerusalem community offered a compromise. Those Gentiles who wanted to become Christian and interact with the Jewish members of the Christian community need only follow the customs proper to resident aliens in Israel. Thus the so-called apostolic decree of Acts 15 directs: "For it has seemed good to the Holy Spirit and to us to lay upon you [Gentiles who want to be Christians] no greater burden than these necessary things: that you abstain from what has been sacrificed to idols [see Lev. 17:8–9] and from blood [see Lev. 17:10–12] and from what is strangled [see Lev. 17:13–16] and from unchastity [Lev. 18:1–23]. If you keep yourselves from these, you will do well. Farewell" (Acts 15:28–29). What this decree required was a minimum set of purity rules to be observed by Gentile Christians so that they might interact "in Christ" with Jewish Christians. The apostolic administrative board in Jerusalem, rather than the Jerusalem elites of Israel, now sanctions this sort of interpretation of Torah.

However, people like Paul believed that the purity rules of Israel—raised to the rank of law and sanctioned by administrative authority—are no longer binding "in Christ." As we have seen in the section on marriage strategy, Paul reverts to custom. Christian purity rules will henceforth derive from the interaction of Christians "in Christ" rather than from previous biblical injunctions. These interactions become the new norms for situating persons and things in their proper places. Just as Paul never cites any Torah norm as law, as legally binding, so too he never considers anything previously sacred as binding in sacred fashion for Christians. For when Paul talks of access to God, of what is sacred to God, he and his communities never adopt and adapt anything considered to be sacred, holy, or sacral to God by their contemporaries, both Jewish and Greek. As we have seen above, such sacred, holy, or sacral items include the Temple, the organization of the people (the worshiping community), sacrifice, sacred personnel, and sacred times and seasons. How does Paul and the post-Pauline tradition after him speak about these areas?

1) *Temple:* For Christians of the Pauline tradition, the Jerusalem Temple was no longer a specific, designated area of sacred space. Rather, the Temple, or more specifically, the sanctuary itself, was the gathering of Christians who formed the body of Christ filled with the Spirit. They together were the "temple of the Holy Spirit" (1 Cor. 6:19; see 1 Cor. 3:16–17) or "the temple of the living God" (2 Cor. 6:16). It is always the holy group, never the individual, that is the Temple of God and the body of Christ. After all, we are dealing with dyadic personalities.

2) *Organization of the People:* Purity lines now consisted only of a distinction between inside and outside. The lines deriving from social status, sexual roles, and ethnicity were leveled (Gal. 3:28; 1 Cor. 12:13; Col. 3:11). People were either "in Christ" or they were not. However, openness to outsiders and concern for their opinion of the group was important. The symbolic passage from outside to inside was marked by the rite of baptism (much as circumcision marked entry into Israel, e.g., Col. 2:11–12). Thus, as the author of Ephesians tells Christian Gentiles, "you are no longer strangers and sojourners [the resident aliens of Judaism], but you are fellow citizens with the saints and members of the household of God, built upon the foundation of the apostles and prophets, Christ Jesus himself being the cornerstone, in whom the whole structure is joined together and grows into a holy temple in the Lord; in whom you also are built into it for a dwelling place of God in the Spirit" (Eph. 2:19–22; read also 1 Peter 2:4–10).

3) *Sacrifice:* For Christians, sacrifice to God symboling patron-client relationship and reciprocity is no longer anything animal or vegetable. Rather, sacrifice is Christian prayer (a way of influencing the patron) and activity (a way of revealing the God you believe in, hence an honoring or glorifying of God). In other words, Christians' sacrifice consists in their common prayer or conduct (read 1 Thess. 5:19–21; Rom. 12:1; 15:16; Col. 3:16–17; Eph. 5:2,15–20; 1 Peter 1:17; 2:4–10; James 1:27). The idea of interpreting Jesus' death as a sacred sacrifice in terms of Jewish Temple ritual is rare in the New Testament, found mainly in the letter to the Hebrews (which you might read in this connection). Rather infrequently, Jesus' death is interpreted as the sacrifice of the Passover lamb (1 Cor. 5:7 and perhaps John 19:14).

4) *Personnel:* The various titles given to Christian leaders all derived from the non-sacred sphere of the Jewish and Greek first-century world. This means that no Christian leader bore a "clerical" or "religious" sacred

title. "Apostle" means authorized messenger; "bishop" means supervisor, overseer, superintendent, especially of fiscal matters; "presbyter" means elder, a senior member, a senior in the faith, perhaps; "deacon" means table-waiter, an establishment's servant. Further, such personnel are appointed to tasks (in Latin "ordain" means to appoint to a job); they are not consecrated or set apart for the sacred like pagan and Jewish priests (e.g., Lev. 8:12; 21:8). Since the only lines in the Christian perspective were between inside and outside, all on the inside had ready access to God along with corresponding obligations toward God—although some had tasks to perform for the group's sake, within the group and perhaps toward outsiders, but not toward God.

5) *Times and Seasons:* If Jesus' death-resurrection ushers in the period in which the future (God's rule, the age to come) is already present in the present, if his saving work is a once-for-all affair (1 Cor. 5:7–8), then all times are now sacred for those on the inside. Hence there is no need to "observe days, and months, and seasons, and years" (Gal. 4:10).

Thus, while the early Christians of the Pauline tradition (and there were others not of this tradition, as Acts 15 indicates) rejected what their contemporaries considered sacred, holy, or sacral to God, they did in fact consider their group to be like a temple, hence a holy, consecrated body of people. Their task relative to purity lines was twofold: (1) to keep this body free from what did not fit "in Christ" and (2) to interact at the margins of the body in such a way that it would please God, hence on the basis of the attitudes and actions rooted "in Christ." The Pauline Christian inside/outside model overlays zones A and C of the previous model and places zone B at the margins of the whole, as follows:

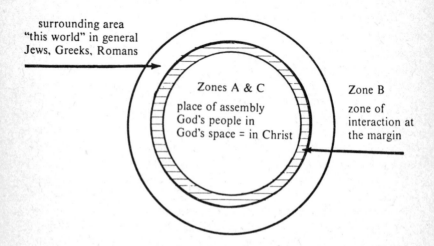

Or in terms of the previous vertical Temple model:

Outside: Space of this world of people often hostile to God in Christ	"This world" of Jews, Greeks, and Romans based on law and political authority
Zone B: Zone of interaction God and the world	Christian activity which is the same as Christian sacrifice
Inside—Zones A and C: Place of assembly and God's space overlap	The Christian group of saints, holy churches, a temple, the body of Christ based on Christian custom

Keeping the social body free of what did not fit "in Christ" was normally a matter of rejecting behavior that was not as good as the best in the cultural norms of the day (e.g., 1 Cor. 5:1 on expelling a community member who marries in a deviant way). It also required rejection of those who sought to compromise the new existence "in Christ" by separating zones A and C, that is, by urging requirements that more befitted previous existence "in Israel" than existence "in Christ" (e.g., Gal. 5:2–12). On the other hand, interaction with "this world" at the margins, the place where Christian sacrifice or sanctification was focused, had concern for neighbor as top priority. In general, it required behavior that was honorable and proper in the Greco-Roman world (e.g., Rom. 13:1–7 on respect for the emperor, paying taxes, and the like). In particular, it required interactions with the sacral world of Jews and Greeks in such a way that concern for neighbor be maintained while the inside of the body not be infected. As a general principle, so long as a person remained in the group, in the body, he or she was holy, consecrated to God along with those embedded in that person. Thus the presumably minor children of Christian parents as well as unbelieving partners married to Christians along with their offspring, are holy (1 Cor. 7:14–15). Presumably, the holiness of the Christian group is more powerful than the uncleanness outside of it; in fact, it is capable of rendering it holy. Hence, so is the holiness of a Christian marriage partner in face of the uncleanness of a non-Christian spouse. All this is due to the ready presence of God made available by the holiness of Jesus Christ, in whom Christians are.

Further, relative to food and times, Paul could say: "I know and am persuaded in the Lord Jesus that nothing is unclean in itself" (Rom. 14:14). The reason for this is that a new set of purity rules takes the place of the old set, and in the new set there is no room for the unclean. However, while everything and everyone in the body is clean, this by no means signifies that the social body of Christians and their actions are morally irrelevant. In other words, just because a Christian did something did not make it good. And whatever a Christian did was not automatically good provided he had good intentions. The heart counts highly, that is true, but so does the action. Both actions and motives count—and this both for the social body and for the individual who replicates the social body. Thus, while nothing is unclean for the Christian, at the margins where one interacts with people who believe in clean and unclean, the perceptions of others must be taken into consideration and respected. This holds for interactions with Jews and pagans (1 Cor. 10:17–19) as well as with one's fellow Christians. Paul's advice for behavior at the margins of the group is: "Give no offense to Jews or to Greeks or to the church of God" (1 Cor. 10:32). However, the most frequent problems Paul alludes to deal with offenses against one's fellow Christians of Jewish background at the individual level, the personal level that replicates the social level. Here as at the social level, neighbor has priority. Hence, "if your brother [fellow Christian] is being injured by what you eat, you are no longer walking in love. Do not let what you eat cause the ruin of one for whom Christ died. . . . it is right not to eat meat or drink wine or do anything that makes your brother stumble' (Rom. 14:15,21; see also 1 Cor. 8:7–13). And if some Christians of Jewish background still resonate with symbolic times, that too need not be a problem provided that "he who observes the day, observes it in honor of the Lord" (Rom. 14:6). In sum, care and concern for one's fellow Christian has priority (1 Cor. 13, where "love" means care and concern for another).

Much of the practical advice in Paul and the other New Testament letters is about making the margins of the group sharper and clearer. Emphasis is on firming up the focus of the group toward the center of the social body. The customs developed and shared in these early Christian, non-Palestinian communities would eventually lead to more complex purity structures in the Christian churches of the second and third centuries and later, not too different in arrangement from that of first-century Palestinian urban, elite Judaism.

Summary

This chapter deals with purity rules, with the way social groups mark off persons and things, time and space. Purity rules enable us to situate the elements of our environment, including ourselves, in such a way that the order facilitates our making sense of our experiences of persons, things, time, and space. Purity rules point out what or who is out of place, out of phase. A subset of purity rules deals with the sacred and the non-sacred, with relations of exclusivity, with the person, things, times, and spaces with which we personally resonate, and those beyond our immediate concern. Just as we have sacred and profane, so by analogy does God. Post-exilic Judaism portrayed God's sacredness in terms of classes of persons through marriage, in terms of space in Temple worship, and in terms of persons and things in sacrifice. The Christian movement, set under way by the death-resurrection of Jesus, had to come to terms with the purity rules of Israel because purity rules, as Jesus' criticisms indicated, likewise symbol the model of God which one believes in. Christians, with their new model of God deriving from the experience of Jesus, reassessed all that was sacred to their contemporary cultures and began to establish new rules for the sacred based upon their group as analogous to a temple, or holy space/people with immediate access to God in Christ.

Testing the Hypothesis

Once more, throughout the chapter I have made reference to a large number of biblical passages which are not quoted in the text. So the first step toward validating or invalidating the models presented here is for you to read all the texts cited in the chapter. As you read the texts, judge whether they fit the model or not. Can you think of some other model by means of which the texts might make better sense? What happens when the texts are interpreted in terms of American purity rules or in terms of our Western traditional understanding of the sacred?

For the Old Testament, a way to test the model is to read carefully through Leviticus 1—4 to determine the meaning of the various sacrifices:
—What sort of sacrifices does each of these chapters deal with?
—Note the types of animals involved as well as their ranking. Who could afford the highest ranking animals; who the lowest?
—Note that in each animal sacrifice, the blood is first poured out and sprinkled around the altar and at the door of the Tent of Meeting (in the first century, the sanctuary building or the porch of the Holy Place). Why? What does blood mean (see Lev. 7:26; 17:11–12)? Why does blood have this meaning?
—Note that the carcass is then divided into two: one portion consisting of the fat and some attached organs, the other consisting of whatever is left. The fat (and attached organs) is always part of the offering, to be burned on the altar. It symbols power, vigor, vitality, hence prosperity, and it too is prohibited to men (see Lev. 7:22–23). Why? Whatever is left is the residue; how is that treated?
—Cereal offerings are not to contain leaven or honey (Lev. 2:11) because they ferment. Fermenting is clearly a process of oozing or spreading beyond given boundaries. Why would this be forbidden in the Temple sacrifice?

In the New Testament, the following passages speak of holy, hallowed, saint, and the like; they all contain the Greek word *hagios* and might be translated variously. Look up the passages and, on the basis of the models, determine why the person or object is considered holy:

Matt. 4:5; 7:6; 24:15; 27:52,53; Mark 1:24; 6:20; 8:38; Luke 1:35,49,70,72; 2:23; 4:34; 9:26; John 6:69; Acts 3:14,21; 4:27,30; 6:13; 7:33; 9:13,32,41; 10:22; 26:10; Rom. 1:2,7; 7:12; 8:27; 11:16; 12:1,13; 15:25,26,31; 16:2,15,16; 1 Cor. 1:2; 3:17; 6:1,2,19; 7:14,34; 14:33; 16:1,15,20; 2 Cor. 1:1; 8:4; 9:1, 12; 13:12; Eph. 1:1,4,15,18; 2:19,21; 3:5,8,18; 4:12; 5:3,27; 6:18; Phil. 1:1; 4:21,22; Col. 1:2,4,12,22,26; 3:12; 1 Thess. 3:13; 5:26,27; 2 Thess. 1:10; 1 Tim. 5:10; 2 Tim. 1:9; Philemon 5,7; 1 Peter 1:15,16; 2:5,9; 3:5; 2 Peter 1:18; 2:21; 3:2,11.

In the foregoing passages, I omitted all mention of the Holy Spirit. Given the model of the holy, what would Holy Spirit mean?

—The following passages deal with the process of making holy, that is, sanctification or sanctifying. Do the models in the text help explain what such passages might mean?

Sanctification: Rom. 6:19,22; 1 Cor. 1:30; 1 Thess. 4:3,4,7; 2 Thess. 2:13; 1 Tim. 2:15; 1 Peter 1:2. *To sanctify:* Matt. 6:9; 23:17,19; Luke 11:2; John 10:36; 17:17,19; Acts 20:32; 26:18; Rom. 15:16; 1 Cor. 1:2; 6:11; 7:14; Eph. 5:26; 1 Thess. 5:23; 1 Tim. 4:5; 2 Tim. 2:21; 1 Peter 3:15 ("Reverence in the R.S.V. is from the Greek "sanctify").

A Theological Conclusion

The careful study of the preceding chapters may leave you surprised and wondering. Now, as you listen to the New Testament authors and the people presented in their texts, you will probably find their concerns about honor and shame, dyadic personality, limited good, defensive marriage, and purity rules quite irrelevant to our everyday modern Western experiences. For example, Americans are for the most part achievement-oriented, keenly aware of limitless good, competitive and individualistic in marriage strategies, with purity rules focused pragmatically upon individual relations and individual success. Other Westerners have similar characteristics.

The anthropological models we have considered are meant primarily to help you differentiate your cultural experiences and perceptions from those in the New Testament. After all, Christianity in its origins is a Middle-Eastern, Mediterranean movement, and if it made direct sense in that cultural form in our own context, we might rightly suspect the New Testament of being a twentieth century forgery. We have a feel for these things; for example, the non-American reader of this contemporary text will know he or she is reading an American book. And if it is strange and unfamiliar at times, how much stranger must be a document from the first-century Mediterranean world.

You might now better appreciate the theological problem that has faced Christianity over the past two millennia. That theological problem has been and continues to be how to make known the Good News of Jesus in terms of the ever-kaleidoscoping cultural scripts that cover the world like a crazy quilt. It is all too easy to read into the New Testament and make do with a Jesus in our own image and likeness. The New Testament thus serves as a veritable Rorschach inkblot, with Jesus coming across as a universal polymorph, a chameleon figure standing for and legitimating whatever individuals and groups choose to do "in his name"—from a local fundamentalist commune to a worldwide church.

In traditional Christian belief, Jesus of Nazareth, God's Messiah, is the concrete historical instance of the union of the divine and the human. This historical union, called the Incarnation, took place in time and space, within a particular set of cultural norms and presuppositions. The problem with a fundamentalism that is interested only in what the Bible says—and not in what it means in terms of the social context in which it emerged—is that it implicitly denies the Incarnation. It denies the full humanity of the God-man, Jesus. It implicitly denies that Jesus was like us in all things save sin. You might reread the introductory chapter with its presuppositions and check out what it means to be "like us" in terms of our cultural makeup.

This book is meant to help in understanding the New Testament writings. If those writings are to resonate in our different cultural context, if faith is to be held responsibly, then theology will have to carry out its work of articulating the culture-bond, original symbols of the primordial Christian movement in terms of the clearest language and models that it can find in the cultures in which it is to be expressed, understood, and lived out.

Bibliography

This bibliography is selective in the sense that it contains references only to the main sources of information used in the preparation of this book.

Chapter 1

Halliday, M. A. K. *Language as a Social Semiotic: The Social Interpretation of Language and Meaning.* Baltimore: University Park Press, 1978.

Kluckhohn, Richard, ed. *Culture and Behavior: Collected Essays of Clyde Kluckhohn.* New York: Free Press, 1965.

Knudson, S. J. *Culture in Retrospect: An Introduction to Archaeology.* Chicago: Rand McNally, 1978.

Langness, L. L. *The Study of Culture.* San Francisco: Chandler & Sharp, 1974.

Leach, Edmund. *Culture and Communication: The Logic by Which Symbols Are Connected.* Cambridge: Cambridge University Press, 1976. See especially pp. 1–24.

Malina, Bruce J. "What Are the Humanities: A Perspective for the Scientific American." In *The Humanities and Public Life,* edited by William L. Blizek, pp. 34–47. Lincoln, Nebraska: Word Services Publishing Company, 1978.

Miller, George A. and Johnson-Laird, Philip N. *Language and Perception.* Cambridge, Mass.: Harvard University Press, 1976.

Novak, Michael. *Ascent of the Mountain, Flight of the Dove: An Invitation to Religious Studies.* 2nd ed. New York: Harper & Row, 1978.

Chapter 2

Bourdieu, Pierre. "The Sentiment of Honour in Kabyle Society." In *Honour and Shame: The Values of Mediterranean Society,* edited by J. G. Peristiany, pp. 191–241. Chicago: University of Chicago Press, 1966. The whole of this volume is appropriate to this chapter.

Kaufman, Gershen. "The Meaning of Shame: Toward a Self-Affirming

Identity." *Journal of Counseling Psychology* 21:568–574. On shame in United States culture.

Pitt-Rivers, Julian. *The Fate of Shechem or the Politics of Sex: Essays in the Anthropology of the Mediterranean.* Cambridge: Cambridge University Press, 1977. See especially pp. 1–17.

Chapter 3

De Geradon, Bernard. "L'homme a l'image de Dieu." *Nouvelle Revue Theologique* 80:683–695.

Geertz, Clifford. " 'From the Native's Point of View': On the Nature of Anthropological Understanding." In *Meaning and Anthropology,* edited by Keith H. Basso and Henry A. Selby, pp. 221–237. Albuquerque: University of New Mexico Press, 1977.

Selby, Henry A. *Zapotec Deviance: The Convergence of Folk and Modern Sociology.* Austin: University of Texas Press, 1974.

Stendahl, Krister. "The Apostle Paul and the Introspective Conscience of the West." *Harvard Theological Review* 56:199–215.

Chapter 4

Potter, Jack M.; Diaz, May N.; and Foster, George M., eds. *Peasant Society: A Reader.* Boston: Little, Brown & Co., 1967. The introductory articles to the sections of this book are all appropriate for the N. T. social world.

Scott, James C. *The Moral Economy of the Peasant.* New Haven: Yale University Press, 1976.

Sjoberg, Gideon. *The Preindustrial City: Past and Present,* Glencoe, New York: Free Press, 1960.

Wolf, Eric R. *Peasants.* Englewood Cliffs, N. J.: Prentice-Hall, 1966.

Chapter 5

Bohannan, Paul. "The Differing Realms of the Law." In *The Social Organization of Law,* edited by Donald Black and Maureen Mileski, pp. 306–317. New York: Academic Press, 1973.

Derrett, J. Duncan M. "The Disposal of Virgins." In his *Studies in the New Testament,* vol. 1, pp. 184–192. Leiden: E. J. Brill, 1977.

Diamond, Stanley. "The Rule of Law Versus the Order of Custom." In *The*

Social Organization of the Law, edited by Donald Black and Maureen Mileski, pp. 318–341. New York: Academic Press, 1973.

Fitzmyer, Joseph A. "The Matthean Divorce Texts and Some New Palestinian Evidence." *Theological Studies* 37:197–226.

Peristiany, J. G., ed. *Mediterranean Family Structure.* Cambridge: Cambridge University Press, 1976.

Pitt-Rivers, Julian. *The Fate of Shechem or the Politics of Sex: Essays in the Authropology of the Mediterranean.* Cambridge: Cambridge University Press, 1977. See especially pp. 126–171.

Williams, Robin M., Jr. *American Society: A Sociological Interpretation.* 3rd ed. New York: Knopf, 1970. See pp. 47–98 on United States marriage norms.

Chapter 6

Douglas, Mary. *Purity and Danger: An Analysis of Concepts of Pollution and Taboo.* London: Routledge and Kegan Paul, 1966.

———. "Deciphering a Meal." *Daedalus* 101:61–81.

Jeremias, Joachim. *Jerusalem in the Time of Jesus: An Investigation into Economic and Social Conditions During the New Testament Period.* Philadelphia: Fortress Press, 1969.

Leach, Edmund. *Culture and Communication: The Logic by Which Symbols Are Connected.* Cambridge: Cambridge University Press, 1976. See especially pp. 81–93.

Acknowledgments

Some of the material in chapters 3 and 4 has appeared in different form in two articles: "Limited Good and the Social World of Early Christianity," *Biblical Theology Bulletin,* vol. 8, no. 4 (1978), pp. 162–176, and "The Individual and the Community—Personality in the Social World of Early Christianity," *Biblical Theology Bulletin,* vol. 9, no. 3 (1979), pp. 126–138, and is used here with permission of the publisher.

The two Venn diagrams in chapter 6, from Mary Douglas' "Deciphering a Meal," are reprinted by permission of *Daedalus,* Journal of the American Academy of Arts and Sciences, Cambridge, Massachusetts. Winter 1972, "Myth, Symbol, and Culture."

Index of Biblical
(and Apocryphal) Passages

General Index